ALWAYS ROOM FOR MORE

Walking Through Open Doors

By

Ann L. McKinney

Dedication

This book is dedicated to Dale Thomas,
who is the love of my life and
my partner in this wonderful chaos we fondly
call,
"Our Family."

Acknowledgments

I would like to thank my parents, Cecil and Marcia, and my in-laws, Jiggs and Ginger, as well as my extended family. Your support has been invaluable. Thank you also to anyone and everyone who has ever helped us fundraise for an adoption, donated to our adoption expenses, babysat, prepared a meal, sent a card, filled my van with groceries, prayed for us, or even just gave me a smile of encouragement. Please know that it blessed my family!

I also want to acknowledge the children who don't have a chapter in this book but still touched me and forever changed my heart: Phillip, Wondemagnet, LeeLee, Bryshawn, Jamarion, Alberto & JeanBerto, Melanie, Jeudy, Ru, Jhoney, Luna, YouYou, Lizzie, Kirtus, John, & Kory, Charissa, MeiMei, NuiNui, Shergeline, Brandon Y, Abeynah, Jamison, Irina, William, Yura, Ippei, Ty, Takahiro, Welbie, Lexie, Shaz, Habel, Myshawn, Toki, Shunichi, Kacey, Jaydyn, Zach, Grace, and all the other beautiful kiddos in my life. I love you all!

Some names have been changed to protect the identity of the people in the story.

Preface

Everywhere we go, we attract attention. Maybe it's because there are so many of us. Maybe it's because there are so many races represented in our family. Maybe it's unusual to see so many boys with hand differences or a family with two children who use wheelchairs. Maybe it's just the fact that we travel everywhere in a big ole' rattling shuttle bus! Regardless of why people stare at us, they sure do!

It used to bother me. Now I see it as an opportunity. I smile, nod, and will usually attempt to start up a conversation with the ones who stare. Most people want to ask questions but don't want to offend or embarrass us. I would prefer questions over stares, and I think most of our children would agree.

The question that Dale and I are asked most often is "**Why?**" People don't understand **why** we would want fifteen children. They don't understand why we would give up the life we could have to be parents to all these kids. Most people in our age group are busy traveling the world, pursuing interesting hobbies, or enjoying an empty nest. People don't understand why we would willingly choose to parent children who will need lifelong care and constant medical attention. They don't see or understand the beauty in serving and obeying. They feel like we are missing out on what the world has to offer us.

Dale and I have several answers to that "Why" question. First of all, we do love children. They bring us joy (except when they all have homework at the same time), and we truly love the constant interaction and activity of a large family. We don't ever have to worry about being bored in our household! But the biggest reason our family looks the way it does is because it represents an act of obedience to our Lord Jesus. As you will read in each chapter of this book, we truly believe that each child in our family was destined to be with us. God called us to step out in faith and pursue these children. Our family would not be complete with even one of them missing.

Adopting so many children has stretched our faith, tested our patience, and pushed our perseverance to the very limit. And it certainly has put a strain on our budget! But the realization that our crazy family is pleasing to the Lord is reward enough, and the smiles and joy our children bring us is a bonus.

Our family, the family God created, has given us the opportunity to share Christ with total strangers. It has encouraged others to adopt, and many orphans have come home to forever families because of the influence of my beautiful children. And because of our family— considering the places we have been and the activities in which we have participated—our life has been one giant adventure. My life is fuller and more exciting than I ever dreamed it would be. I should also add that I have done more laundry and changed more diapers than I ever thought was humanly possible! But I've enjoyed (almost) every minute of it!

So here it is. This is the story of our journey into God's perfect will for our family, into a life more beautiful than I could ever have hoped for. It's the chance to share my children's fascinating, unique, and memorable birth and adoption stories with the world to encourage adoption, family, and obedience. I pray you enjoy our story. Through it all, I have learned that there is Always Room for More on this great adventure!

Children are a heritage from the Lord, offspring a reward from Him. Like arrows in the hands of a warrior are children born in one's youth. Blessed is the man whose quiver is full of them. They will not be put to shame when they contend with their opponents in court. (Psalm 127:3-5)

Copyright

All Scripture taken from the "NIV" HOLY BIBLE, NEW INTERNATIONAL VERSION. Copyright 1973, 1978, 1984 by International Bible Society. Used by permission of Zondervan Publishing House.

Send Hope Publishing
www.SendHopePublishing.com

Content

Chapter 1

In the Beginning...

Children were never on my radar. I was the oldest of four and spent a lot of time babysitting and helping my mother care for my younger siblings.

My mother was a full-time homemaker who enjoyed sewing. Most of the clothing I wore as a child was hand-made with love by my mother. My father worked for Firestone, building tires, and put in many hours of overtime to make sure he could adequately provide for our family. I have a sister, Amy, who is four years younger than me. A fiery redhead, she inherited my mother's love for sewing and crafts. Travis is my only brother, five years younger than me; being the only boy in our family, we spoiled him pretty well! My baby sister is Susan, who was born when I was ten, and she and I share our love for animals and children.

As I got older, I babysat for many children in our neighborhood, and while I liked them, I always thought of all of the trouble they caused their parents, and how expensive they were.

Animals, however, I loved. I had many pets throughout my childhood, including dogs, cats, hamsters, guinea pigs, mice, birds, fish, and horses. Animals showed me an unconditional love that people generally didn't possess. People held grudges, pouted, and struggled with forgiveness. People had hurt me, and I had hurt them. In my mind, it was just too complicated. So, many of my fondest childhood memories do not involve people but are of time spent with my beloved dog, Rambo, or trudging through miles of forest trails on my sweet horse, Lacey. Those two were my best friends.

My relationship with Jesus was also a roller coaster. I was raised in a wonderful Baptist church where I was taught God's love from the day I was born. I loved to sing in the children's choir, I was very involved in youth missions, and vacation Bible school was my favorite thing in the world. My parents modeled Christ exceptionally well for me. They served Christ by teaching, donating, and building relationships with those who were struggling.

I accepted Christ as my Savior at Lake Salateeska Camp in southern Illinois the summer I turned twelve. But it was hard to hold

2

on to my faith. As time passed, many girls in my youth group became catty and mean. Youth group became more about how expensive your clothes were and who you were dating instead of how you were living for Jesus. I slipped. And the more I dated, the more I slipped. I still loved Jesus and prayed every day, but I was certainly not living for Him. He was always there, however, just waiting for me to come back.

The day I met my husband, Dale, I was walking my dog with a friend through the playground of an elementary school. My family had just moved to the community, and I was still figuring it all out. I had caused my parents quite a bit of trouble, which prompted them to move us out of the city and into the country, where my mother had been raised. I was angry, a bit lost, and uncomfortable in my new surroundings.

Dale was playing basketball with a bunch of other guys. I distinctly remember them all being sweaty and smelly, as it was sweltering that day. Of all the guys playing basketball, he was the only one who seemed to notice me. He stepped back from the game to walk toward me.

"Hello, I'm Dale. Are you new in the neighborhood?" he said as he approached.

"I am. We moved in last week. I'm still getting used to the idea of being a country gal," I responded. We both laughed. He was friendly and had a good sense of humor, and although it certainly was not "love at first sight," I did like him and thought he would make a really good friend in my forced relocation.

Throughout high school, Dale and I remained friends. I dated many different boys, most of whom were not good for me. Looking back, I realize that I had this weird "need" to always have a boyfriend. And it was even better if he was a boyfriend my parents did not approve of! I was that typical teenage girl rebelling against her parents, who were nothing but good and fair to her. I wish I could change those days for the sake of my parents, but I also know it was all a part of God's plan to help develop me into the person I am today. But I was quite a jerk to my family.

Dale and I had one common denominator. Her name was Michele, and she was an interesting young lady of whom I became quite fond. She was not very well-liked. In fact, she was bullied and taken advantage of on many occasions. She struggled with social settings, had a bad temper, and did not care what others thought or said about her. I envied her because I wished that I, too, could shut out the negative voices and just be me. Michele and I became friends not long after I moved to the area.

Dale was one of the very few people in the entire school who was kind to Michele; I noticed that immediately. He teased her, but not in a mean way at all, more like the way a big brother teases his little sister. She teased him right back, and they genuinely seemed to like each other, despite what anyone else might think. They also had something in common with me; they both loved Jesus and were struggling with how to live that out in the dreadful teenage years.

Just before our high school graduation, Michele got pregnant. She and her boyfriend decided to get married at the courthouse in a quiet ceremony. Michele was my first experience with pregnancy, and it freaked me out to see someone my own age getting ready to be a mother! Michele gave birth to a beautiful baby boy whom she named Michael after her older brother, who had passed away at birth. Little Michael was so cute! I spent many hours with Michele and did my best to help her as she leaped headfirst into motherhood.

And then, a tragedy. I was singing in the choir one Sunday morning, and just after our last song, our pastor asked the congregation if there were any prayer requests. A woman stood up and asked for prayer for the family of my friend, Michele, as she had been found dead in her home that morning. I could not believe what I was hearing! No-way; Michele was my age! It must have been a mistake. I got up from my seat in the choir and went straight to my car. This was before the age of cell phones, so I drove home in a panic and called Mark, Michele's husband. It was true. Michele was dead. She was found dead on the couch when Mark returned home from work. The coroner later determined she had died of an aneurysm that had burst in her head, possibly related to the strain of childbirth on her body. I was devastated; Michele was my only close friend. She knew more about me than anyone, even my parents. She left behind a newborn baby boy. And me.

Michele's visitation was a horrible experience for me. Almost every student from our school was there, and most of them were crying. To be honest, it made me ill. They didn't care about her! They were not even nice to her! But as I look back, I wonder if maybe that is why they were crying. Maybe they finally realized that she died without hearing a kind or encouraging word from most of them. I hope in my heart that is why they cried. Dale was there, and he was one of the few who I thought was truly mourning.

Michele's mother sought me out to talk with me. After some small talk, I asked the question that had been weighing heavily on my mind.

"Mrs. Grandel," I asked, "What will happen to baby Michael? Will his father be able to raise him?"

Mrs. Grandel responded, "No, that's not possible, so we are considering all of our options. What about you; would you consider adopting and raising Michael?"

Me? Oh no, I was eighteen years old with lots of life ahead of me, a broken heart, and absolutely no experience with being a momma.

"I'm sorry, but I don't think that is a very realistic option for me," I heard myself tell her.

The conversation I had with her lingers in my mind to this very day. I wonder if my answer came from a selfish heart. What if I had said yes? What if I would have raised that beautiful, sweet baby? What if?

After the visitation, several of my classmates were deciding where they could have a keg party. Seriously. I couldn't believe how quickly their grief dissipated as they planned a drinking binge. I don't remember exactly what I said to them, but I do know that it involved pure anger, some screaming, and me running from the funeral home in tears. Dale followed me out. He took me to Dairy Queen, bought me a blizzard, and tried to soothe my broken heart. It was probably the most sincere, caring, and romantic thing any man had ever done for me. He did not have ulterior motives; he just cared. I felt something in my heart for him that night. Something beautiful and scary at the same time!

Dale and I became best friends. I was dating a man that I was working with at the time, but in my heart, I knew that relationship was wrong. Dale and I began going to movies and Christian concerts together, and I followed him and his band around like a groupie. I liked him so very much! I wasn't sure I loved him, though, and I was still dating my coworker. And there was yet another issue: Dale **loved** children and wanted to have **lots** of them. That totally freaked me out, but in no way could I deny that something was going on in my heart, something I had not felt before. I so often thought I was in love with the boy I was dating. Now, after feeling this, I realized it was very different.

I broke up with my boyfriend and decided I needed a career. Since animals were such a huge part of my life, I chose to go to pet-grooming school. So, in the fall of 1986, I headed to the New York School of Dog Grooming in midtown Manhattan.

Culture shock! I don't ever remember seeing so many cars, people, and chaos all around me. Everyone was in a hurry, and rarely did anyone smile. The part that was the hardest for me was the homelessness. This was the first time I got to meet and know people who actually lived and slept on the sidewalks. I grew especially fond of a young woman who slept on the steps of the grooming school. She kept a small kitten on a string, and each night I took her a soda to drink and a morsel of food for her kitten. She touched my heart with her simplicity and her appreciation for anything that was given to her.

Dale called me often, and we wrote letters to stay in touch. I slipped once again and began dating a boy from school. However, after my time with Dale—and working diligently on my relationship with God—I was convicted almost immediately that it was wrong, so I ended it as quickly as it began.

My trade school was a nine-month program, and I could not wait to see Dale again when I got home. We were both happy to see each other! I waited each night to hear his squeaky old blue Ford Fairlane as he drove past my house on his way home from work. Sometimes he would leave candy or a note in my car. I realized that I could not fight it anymore; I was falling in love with this crazy red-haired man who wanted a huge family.

Just a few weeks after I returned from New York, Dale came calling.

"I would love to see you tonight. I have something exciting to discuss with you," he said. I could tell it was serious by his tone and by the nervousness in his voice. I got scared because, at this point, we were not dating but were just best friends. I was afraid of commitment. Looking back, I'm not sure why I was so scared. I never took dating seriously in the past, but I knew in my heart this was very different.

Dale picked me up and we drove around. "Ann, I have made a decision about my future, and it affects you." I held my breath as he continued.

"I'm joining The Jesus People and will be traveling the country with them."

Dale had made a new, firm commitment to the Lord, and he planned to evangelize all over the Midwest. He would be traveling with this group, assisting with tent revivals, singing, and sharing Christ with a boldness and enthusiasm he never had before.

I was shocked. This was not at all the news I was expecting, and I was not at all sure how to process it. I should have been so happy for him, but instead, I was sad, scared, and almost feeling lost. I tried to smile, but I wanted to cry.

"That is great, Dale," was my disheartened response. Dale took me home, and I began to pray. I never wanted to do anything to keep Dale from following God's calling on his life, but I also felt 100 percent sure that I was part of the calling God had for him!

The next time Dale and I went out, I couldn't hold it in. I told him that I thought we were supposed to be together, and then I asked him to marry me! It was crazy. I couldn't believe I heard those words come out of my mouth. He looked shocked and overwhelmed, and at first, I thought he was going to throw me out of the car and drive away! But instead, we shared our first kiss. And then he asked me if I loved him. I told him I did. We were both so excited, and he shared with me that he had been feeling the exact same way for many years.

11

We went to find our beloved Pastor Randy, who was mowing grass at the very same elementary school where Dale and I had met. When we told him that we were getting married, he asked who we were marrying. Remember, we were not even dating up to this point! Pastor Randy asked us to have a few more marriage counseling sessions than was normal because of the difference in ideas Dale and I had regarding our family size, and because of our unusual relationship. Dale wanted eight children. I didn't want any. We would just have to wait and see how that played out. I am sure God laughed over this dilemma, and I'm sure He couldn't wait to see my heart change!

We were married on February 27, 1988. It was a beautiful wedding. Somehow, we squeezed over 300 people in our little country church. My mother crafted my wedding dress, spending hours making sure each stitch was perfect, and my grandmother made us her secret recipe "Wedding Punch" that everyone loves. Our siblings stood at the altar with us as bridesmaids and groomsmen. Dale wrote a song as a surprise gift to me and sang it to me during the ceremony. It was a perfect day.

This is how it all began, and we had no idea of the amazing adventure God had planned for us. So, let's get started on the real story!

That is why a man leaves his father and mother and is
united to his wife, and they become one flesh.
(Genesis 2:24)

Chapter 2

Baby Smartie

We were almost three years into our marriage, and life was good. Dale was enrolled in an EMT program at the local college while working both at a hospital and for an ambulance service. I had opened a small pet-grooming business, Groomingdales Pet Center, that had immediately become very successful. I was also showing Tibetan Spaniels all over the Midwest and having much success there as well. Life was good, and I was happy with things just the way they were. But God had a plan for us and didn't give us much choice in the matter!

At first, I was just so very tired, more tired than I should have been, and naps didn't help. And then I realized I had missed that monthly friend. I pushed it to the back of my mind, as I had been faithful in using birth control, so I couldn't possibly be pregnant. Absolutely not. A few weeks later, I began feeling a bit nauseous in the morning and realized that I had missed yet another monthly visitor. I could not be pregnant,

14

right? After all, I wasn't planning on being a mom.

A few days later, I sat on the couch in complete shock, holding a positive pregnancy test. Dale was over the moon excited, and I was still trying to figure out how this had happened. The funniest part of my pregnancy was Dale. He was excited to tell people that I was pregnant, but at the same time, he was embarrassed because then people would know that we had been intimate. Oh, the silly man! I think if we were newly married and hadn't been intimate, that would have been more embarrassing.

The more I prayed, and the more that time went by, the more excited I became with this whole new idea of motherhood. Feeling my baby kick for the first time was an experience I cannot describe; it was pure excitement, knowing this little creature inside me was alive and well. And alive and well she was, as she kicked, jumped, head-butted, and performed somersaults in my womb, over and over, day and night. This little baby was an active one! One fun thing that developed from my pregnancy was an insane craving for Smarties candies. I literally could not get enough of them. Hence, this baby became known as "Baby Smartie." Little did we know how well she would live up to this name.

My pregnancy progressed slowly and uneventfully. My beloved dogs realized they could no longer find a place on my lap. My pants no longer fit. My skin stretched and groaned. But I came to find perfect peace and joy at the idea of becoming a mother. I began to get so excited; I was having a baby! I wondered if Michele had felt this excitement. I wondered how little Michael, who would be four at this point, was doing.

My due date was February 27, which was also our anniversary. It came. And it went. I was not dilated, not effaced. Not even close. My mother told me that the women in our family typically carried their babies well past their due date. Two more weeks went by with no baby, although I began to have small contractions. Finally, on March 18, my doctor decided to admit me to the hospital to begin inducing my baby's delivery.

After twenty-four hours of medication to induce my labor, and a nurse painfully breaking my water, I was only dilated to a two. It was brutal. On top of painful, medically induced contractions, I had a terrible cold and could not breathe out of my nose. I was miserable but excited. And the hours ticked by. And the contractions continued.

On March 19, at 2:00 am, my baby's heart rate began to drop. Not dangerously low, but low enough to cause concern. A team of doctors and nurses talked with Dale and me about the necessity of performing a C-section to deliver our baby. I was scared but also very ready to meet this little acrobat, who was determined to stay put. I was prepped and taken to surgery, with Dale by my side. Once on the surgical table, I began to have severe pain, much worse than a contraction. The pain was so intense it took my breath away. I kept asking the doctors not to touch me until it was finally over. My baby, the acrobat who didn't want to be born, had completely flipped herself breach. Her head had not been engaged in my birth canal this entire time.

Brogan Danielle was born at 3:23 am on March 19. She was beautiful and chubby and bald and mad! And I was a mom.

Brogan was born with a slightly larger head than normal, which made all the doctors freak out, but it was fine. I tell her, to this day, it is because she is so smart. She was also born with her hips dislocated; that was more of a concern. When she was a week old, we were

17

referred to a pediatric orthopedic specialist. Brogan was fitted for a brace, which she was required to wear twenty-four hours a day for the next six months. For many people, it was tricky to figure out how to diaper her around the brace, but since I was not used to diapering a baby, it was easy for me. I simply didn't know any different.

Baby Brogan made me love being a mom. She learned so quick, smiled so easy, talked and walked so soon, and had my heart for animals. I thanked God for using this little sunshine to change my heart for children. I loved this girl and could not imagine my life without her. I was a mom! Now what?

The journey had begun! I had absolutely no idea how God would use my love for this little girl to open my heart to loving children in need, but it was all a part of God's plan.

Sweet little Brogie's hurt her arm,
Sure hope she doesn't lose her charm.
Cute little Brogie's hurt her wrist,
That girl, the boys cannot resist.
Darling Brogie broke her bone,
Won't those tough boys leave her alone?
Remember, little Brogie, what daddy said,
No sympathy kisses or that boy's dead!

(Written after an unusually rough hockey season.)

Chapter 3

Patrick - AKA "Macker"

Brogan was about to have her first birthday. I was so excited to celebrate the birth of my sweet baby girl! But as I busied myself preparing for the party, I began to feel ill. It happened mostly in the evenings, but something was definitely going on. I worked at my grooming salon every day, and by the time I got home each night, I was exhausted. So incredibly tired and nauseous.

Once again, my monthly friend had not visited me on time. But I had been faithfully using birth control, so I could not possibly be pregnant, right? Wrong! The day before Brogan's first birthday, I found out I was pregnant again. Shock, shock, and more shock. And, admittedly, a few tears. Could I really parent two kids and run my business?

Dale was elated! There was no way he could contain this news with all of our family and friends at our house for Brogan's party, so we decided to let everyone know early, even though I was just barely pregnant. We found a board book about being a big sister, wrapped

20

it up, and gave it to Brogan for a birthday gift. And that is how our friends and family found out we were having baby number two.

I had no worries about Brogan being a wonderful big sister. She loved her dogs, her stuffed animals, and her younger cousins. She was a natural nurturer, like her momma, even though I had not fully accepted that role at this point. I secretly hoped for a baby boy, thinking a girl and a boy would complete our family. Dale would be happy with that and would let go of his idea of having a large family.

My second pregnancy was just as easy as my first. I was fully prepared for another long one with a high chance of a C-section, since Brogan was delivered by that method. I had some nausea for the first few months, but it was mild. Grape juice and saltine crackers became my comfort foods, as well as chicken pot pies and cream puffs. I was able to work at my grooming salon right up until the day my baby was born, and my customers loved watching my belly grow.

At this point in our marriage, Dale was working as a paramedic for a local ambulance company. He worked a twenty-four-hour shift, so he was gone frequently through the night. I got lonely and bored at night, and even baby

Brogan and my dear dog and cat friends could not give me the conversation I needed. So, when my mother and sisters invited me to go out for pizza one evening, I jumped at the chance. I was very near my due date at this time.

As we sat at Monical's Pizza, chomping away on breadsticks, the first contraction hit. What on earth? This was a harder contraction than any I ever had with Brogan! They began coming regularly, to the point that I could time them. Since I had never experienced actual labor, I still was not convinced that this was it.

I couldn't even finish my pizza. I had completely lost my appetite. I called Dale.
"Dale, I think I might be in labor!"
"Oh honey, I doubt it; it's probably only Braxton Hicks. Don't worry, you'll be fine."
He was not at all concerned. Part of his EMT training had been in labor and delivery, and he had learned a lot about pre-labor contractions and false labor. He assumed that was what was going on. Mom took me home, and I put Brogan and the dogs to bed and tried to get some sleep.

I soon found myself walking up and down the hallway, however, trying to cope with the ever-increasing contractions.

Finally, at 3:00 am, I called Dale again.

"Dale, this is the real thing. I need to get to the hospital now!"

Again, his response was calm. "Let me see if I can find someone to cover my shift. Hang in there!"

Anxious minutes passed as I waited for his return call, and when it came, the news was not reassuring. He couldn't find anyone to help him out.

I called my momma. "Mom, this baby is coming, I need to get to the hospital, and Dale can't find anyone to cover his shift!"

"I'll be right there!"

Mom came and took me to the hospital, while Dad stayed with Brogan and the pets. At the hospital, the nurses confirmed that I was actually in labor.

My labor was long and hard. It seemed to last forever. I thought for sure I would give birth during the night, but as the sun rose, I was still contracting. Dale was trying his best to comfort me, but I became more and more agitated. Breakfast time came and went. And then, just before lunch, things changed. I had finally reached the pushing stage. I had determined that I would not use any pain medications; I wanted this to be an all-natural childbirth. I was exhausted, but the pushing stage gave me new energy, and I worked hard to get that sweet babe out of my body and into the world.

Our baby Patrick felt like fire as he passed through my birth canal, but he was here, he was perfect, and he was loud. And he was a **boy**! He was smaller than expected, with no hair (just like his sister) and very healthy lungs. Daddy got his son, and I thought we were done. Dale and I thanked God for a beautiful, healthy baby boy. No complications, no drama, just a precious baby boy.

From day one, Patrick has been such a laid-back child. As a baby, he was very happy and rarely cried. He had his favorite toys, his favorite shows, and his favorite blanket. Patrick went through a stage of being a very hyperactive boy, but his energy levels stabilized as a teen. (Thank goodness!) Today is very chill, extremely devoted, and loyal. He's a hard worker and very compassionate. He is my dependable go-to child who is always there for me.

So began life as a mother of two. And I thought I was busy. Ha! This was only the beginning of God's plan for my family. We were far from done.

Patty-Mac, my first-born son,
God made you so cool and fun.
You love to hear your Odyssey tapes,
Your legs are always full of scrapes.
Roller-blading is fun for you,
But I know what you LOVE to do.
You love those mud-fights in the creek,
You go there every single week.
Your hair gets caked with mud and gook,
I like it best when you read a book.

Chapter 4

The Heart Change

The human spirit is the lamp of the Lord
that sheds light on one's inmost being.
(Proverbs 20:27)

What does God find in my heart?
Anything I am hiding?
Anything I need to change?

Dale and I had been Christians most of our lives. We loved Jesus, attended church every Sunday, led Bibles studies, and taught children's classes and led youth services at our church.

But we fell into a trap that a lot (maybe even most) of Christians fall into. We served God on our terms. We served Him when it was easy, when it was already something we were doing, or when we were not inconvenienced. The closer we grew to God, the more we felt like we needed to surrender our lives to Him completely. We needed to let Him take the steering wheel, and we needed to just be the obedient passengers.

Brogan and Patrick were young and needing a lot of me. I was an officer with the Humane Society, which involved many investigations, phone calls, meetings, and last-minute inconveniences. I also showed dogs all over the Midwest, which involved a tremendous amount of my time and money. Dale was consumed with work, music, and holding down the fort when I was off to a dog show. We didn't leave a lot of extra time for God, and the time that we did commit to Him was more out of obligation than spiritual motivation.

Then, at a Lay Witness revival at our church, "it" happened. We gave God our all. Every bit. We both decided then and there to step back and let God show us His path. It was a powerful moment, and one with life-changing consequences.

One struggle I personally had was in regard to animals. I loved animals. I still do. But at this point in my life, they were quickly and solidly consuming me. I began to pray about my animals and what God wanted me to do about my obsession with them. I couldn't just change overnight. But I knew it was wrong for me to spend so much time and money on them when people all around me were in need and suffering, especially children. I understand that this is not how everyone feels, and I would never condemn anyone for loving animals. It was just wrong for me at this point because I loved them to the point that they were my life. They were my god.

I had a very special dog named Doc. I owned his mother, an AKC Champion, and Doc was an amazing show dog with huge potential. He completed his AKC Championship as a puppy and even received a special award for his breed before the age of one. He was the dog that was going to make me noteworthy in the dog-showing world, and I was so excited about him! The thought of not showing him and thus wasting his potential horrified me, as did the idea of selling him. I just didn't know what to do with this little guy.

Well, I didn't have to make that decision. In a cruel twist of fate, a man we had hired to do some drywall work left the gate to our yard open. Doc escaped, and a car hit him. He died in Dale's arms as he rushed him to the vet. It was horrible. I couldn't speak for days. I could barely pray because I felt as though God took this dog from me to get me back on track. I lost all interest in showing dogs; that passion died when Doc died. It was part of my heart change. As time passed, my heart healed, and eventually, I accepted the loss of my beloved Doc. I was able to see clearly how much time and money I had spent showing dogs. God convicted me that He had a different purpose for my time and resources. Okay, God, that issue is gone from me; what's next?

Sometime after Doc died, I was in my grooming salon when *Focus on the Family* had a special program on the radio. This program was about the orphan crisis all over the world, but particularly in China. I listened to every single word, and God moved on my heart in a way I had never felt before. The hosts of this program talked about children housed in orphanages with little food or water and no one to love them. They mentioned the mass graves that were found containing the bodies of children who were missing their organs. Most likely, these were orphans whose organs were harvested. The hosts repeatedly mentioned God's command for us to care for the orphan and the fatherless, and they also issued a bold statement that Christians were closing their eyes while children were suffering and dying.

And then, somehow, in the way only God can, He showed me that the compassion He had given me for animals was now being transformed. Caring for animals had taught me love and nurturing skills. My love for and devotion to animals had become a springboard for what God had planned for me next. God moved on my heart so powerfully right there in my grooming salon! He opened my eyes and my heart to His children who were alone and suffering. CHILDREN! Dying children! Children who had no one to hug them, comfort them, or provide for them. I knew what our next step was. We were going to China, and we were going to adopt one of these babies. The fire was lit in my heart!

Chapter 5

Rosita

After the heart-change I had experienced in my grooming salon, I could not wait to share the news with Dale. Remember, Dale had always wanted a big family, so I knew he would be as excited as I was. And he was! I think he was even more excited than I was.

We began to look online at various adoption agencies that could help us adopt a child from China. And then we received a devastating blow. China had recently changed its policy and would only allow parents without biological children to adopt. I was so upset. I could not understand why God would place this on my heart if it were not a possibility.

We kept digging and found an adoption agency that worked in countries all over the world. We contacted them, and they sent some files of children for us to consider.

One child who won both of our hearts was a beautiful little princess from Colombia. Her name was Rosita, and she was three years old. She was a special needs child and was diagnosed with Hepatitis B. She had black, wavy pigtails and a mischievous grin, and we fell in love. Brogan and Patrick were also excited about having a new sister. This was it; we had found God's will for our family!

Dale and I arranged for a babysitter, and then we gathered up the massive adoption application and headed out to dinner. Our plan was to have a "paperwork" date night. We worked together, finishing both our paperwork and a tasty dinner. Afterward, we went to the mall and purchased Rosita a beautiful little sundress to wear home on the plane.

We finished the adoption application and intake form in record time, and I mailed it to the adoption agency in one big, fat envelope. And then we waited.

A week later, the phone rang.
"Hello, is this Mrs. McKinney?"
"Yes, it is."
"I'm Julia with the adoption agency. We received your application, but I need to inform you that Rosita has been matched with another family."
Tears. No words, only tears.
Really, God? What the heck! We were trying here! We followed Your heart as You led us to China, we followed Your heart as You led

us to Rosita, and both times our hearts were broken. Now what?

Again, I'm sure God smiled as He patiently waited for us to be ready for His plans for our family.

I still think about Rosita, and I still have her photo. I wonder where she is. Is she happy? Does her family teach her about Jesus? Is she here in the United States? In Illinois? I pray for her. I pray that she has an amazing life and that she knows we loved her, even though we never had the honor of meeting her.

When I recall our "paperwork date night," I do have to laugh. We were so naïve. We had no idea what a home study involved. We didn't even know the word *dossier*, and we had no clue about the matching process in international adoption. Oh, the things we had to learn! God was moving, but in His timing.

Wait and See:
I can't wait to see
What the Lord has planned for me.

Wait and pray:
I must wait and pray
To see if today is the day.
Trust and seek:
I'll trust and seek,
Maybe tomorrow, maybe next week.

Wait on you:
I'll wait on you;
Ask me, Lord, and I will do.

Chapter 6

Torren

One day, as I was surfing the web and helping Brogan and Patrick with their homework, I stumbled across an advertisement for foster-care adoption. This was one option Dale and I had never considered, mostly because of all of the horror stories we had heard over the years. It is sad that foster care has such a bad reputation, but it does, especially here in Illinois. Heartbreaking.

The advertisement intrigued me, so I clicked on it and rabbit-trailed through a whole lot of information until I landed on a "Waiting Children" page. This term was new to me, but I soon discovered that it meant the child had been legally cleared for adoption and was now waiting to be found by their forever family.

I scrolled through a lot of faces and felt my heart breaking over the sheer number of kids on this page. And then I saw him.

His name was Torren. He was maybe three or four years old and was wearing a three-piece suit. He had the biggest smile I had ever seen. He was adorable! And also horribly disfigured. He was covered head to toe with awful, dark, deep scars. As I read his profile, I learned that he had been asleep in his crib during a house fire. He was lucky to be alive, but his family could not accept his disability or provide the amount of medical care he now needed. He had already had several reconstructive surgeries but would require many more in the coming years.

I printed out his photo and taped his sweet, smiling face to the front page of my prayer journal. And I prayed. I prayed for him every time I thought of him, which was often. Brogan, Patrick, Dale, and I prayed for him each night at bedtime. I prayed for him to find his family and for his scars to heal; I knew he would have both physical and emotional scars. He needed God's hand to touch his precious body and bring him peace and healing.

After several weeks of our family praying for Torren, I got really brave and called the agency that had posted his information. I had to inquire about him. Although I wasn't sure we were meant to be his family, he felt like a part of me. I sensed a stirring inside; my compassion for this child was off the charts.

Then, the caseworker told me that a family had been found for Torren, and he would be transitioning to their home very shortly. I was overjoyed at hearing this! I felt as though I had a small role in his placement by advocating for him through prayer. I loved this boy I had never met.

Torren, wherever you are, you touched my heart. I pray that you are thriving in the love of your new family. I pray that you have persevered through your surgeries and medical treatments. Please know that this family in Illinois loved you very much and that we prayed for you, and still do. We love you, little man, as does your heavenly Father.

And whoever welcomes one such child in my
name
welcomes me.
(Matthew 18:5

Chapter 7

The Story of Keagan

Dale and I had put adoption on the back burner. It was still in our hearts, but it seemed that each time we tried to move forward, there was a huge roadblock. We kept praying for God to show us His path, and we waited. Waiting is so hard, but during this time, God was growing us into better parents. He was preparing us to parent more children, even those with special needs.

And then along came my friend Stephanie. I didn't even know Stephanie was considering adoption when she announced that she was the proud mother of a newborn, a precious little Hispanic girl named Julia. And a short time later came Ben, a biracial baby boy, who was just as adorable. Stephanie told me that she had utilized the services of an adoption attorney who had difficulty placing minority or special needs children. This intrigued us.

We met with the attorney, Kirsten, who introduced us to a birthmother by the name of Jamie. We spoke to Jamie several times on the phone. She was an intelligent young woman who was facing a crisis pregnancy, and was scared, confused, and overwhelmed. She asked us to parent her unborn son who was due in less than a week, so we quickly prepared to be the parents of a baby boy we had decided to name Solomon James. And then—we never heard from Jamie again. To this day, we do not know what happened to Jamie and baby Solomon. Did she choose to parent him? Did she decide to place him with another family? Did a family member step up and provide a home for him? We have no idea.

To many families, this unfortunate event would have deterred them from pursuing adoption. But we were different. This was not the same as missing out on a China adoption or losing Rosita; this situation motivated us! We heard the anxiety in Jamie's voice, and the anguish she expressed over her crisis pregnancy. God was calling us to step in for these dear, sweet mommas who were facing an unwanted pregnancy, sometimes completely alone. We moved full force into domestic adoption, completing an adoption portfolio and submitting it to several agencies and attorneys.

Soon, a birth mom named Jennifer asked for an interview. Our attorney, Kirsten, had worked with Jennifer before, but she had chosen to parent instead of place. She was a risk, and we knew that. Jennifer was a beautiful, charismatic young lady, and we enjoyed meeting her, as well as her boyfriend Rob and her children. Jennifer could be hard and cold on the outside, but I soon found her sweet, giggly, young soul that was buried behind a strong mask and a need for acceptance. We quickly became friends, and she asked Dale and me to parent her son.

Jennifer did have certain expectations. One day, as we were discussing the upcoming adoption, she looked at me with an expression that could only be described as challenging.

"You know, Ann, I do have some requirements."

I smiled. "I expected that."

"I need you to take me to all my appointments before the baby comes." It wasn't a question.

I paused before answering. My days were quite busy, but… "Sure, I don't think that will be a problem." I actually liked the idea of meeting her doctor and being a part of the prenatal appointments. I just wished she lived closer.

She continued. "And I need you there when the baby is born. I mean, I need you in the room with me, holding my hand. I don't think I can choose adoption for this baby if you are not there to accept him as soon as he is born."

As if she had to ask! I longed to be there when the little guy arrived, but I hadn't dared to bring it up. Now she **wanted** me there! I breathed a silent praise to God.

"And one more thing," she said. "If you're going to adopt my little boy, I need to be able to stay in touch. I want to call you, and you call me, and I want to be a part of his life. He has to know that I love him and only want the best for him." Again, it wasn't really a question.

"Well, Jennifer, I need to talk to Dale about that, but I completely agree that this baby needs all of us in his life. We want him to know his mother, and we surely don't want you to lose contact with him!"

A look of relief flickered across her face, and her smile returned.

A few months later, we got "The Call." Jennifer was in labor! She not-so-nicely told us to get our butts to the hospital ASAP, so off we went. Once we arrived, Jennifer was not very far along in her labor, so Dale made himself comfortable in the waiting room while I rubbed Jennifer's back, got her ice chips, and tried to keep her calm. She was quite an angry woman when she was in labor; the only thing that made her happy was watching horror movies. So, we watched Alfred Hitchcock's *The Birds* while her labor progressed. I think we watched it at least three times, so my memories of Keagan's birth always bring to mind people being attacked by birds.

Keagan's entrance into this world was so amazing. I had given birth to two children, one by C-section and one VBAC, but watching the birth of my newest son was simply incredible! His labor and birth were textbook perfect, without so much as a single complication. He entered our world with a deep breath and then a loud cry. He had a small amount of curly black hair and a much lighter complexion than I was expecting, the perfect combination of his coffee-colored momma and cream-colored daddy. I was the first to hold him, I cut his umbilical cord, and I was the one who comforted him during his first real cry. It was an amazing and beautiful experience that I thank God for all the time. Keagan was perfect!

I was, however, worried about bonding with Keagan. I had bought into the nonsense that not carrying him in my womb would somehow make him not feel like my son. I felt the need to hold him skin on skin, and even learned about breastfeeding a child without first experiencing a pregnancy. But I soon found out that bonding with Keagan was not an issue whatsoever. Our entire family fell madly in love with our little mocha-boy, who was quite a charmer and a flirt at a very young age. He was our son from day one. Blood does not make a family, love does, and we certainly had that.

One lesson I learned through little Keagan was how children regard differences. One afternoon, as Brogan and Patrick were taking turns holding him, a thought occurred to me.

"Hey, you two, have you ever noticed that Keagan's skin is darker than yours? Is that okay with you?"

They both glanced at Keagan then looked up at me, eyes wide.

"What? He has darker skin than us?"

They had never even noticed, and oh, how I wish adults were so color blind! I never mentioned it again.

Keagan is no longer a boy but a man. His beautiful adoption story led us to adopt again, and again, and again. Twelve more times, to be exact. We often joke that our family size is all his fault! He made it so fun and easy. We still have a wonderful relationship with Jennifer and love and appreciate her gift to us in so many ways. She is one of the strongest, bravest women I have met, and she will always be a hero in my eyes. And Keagan, even though he now stands six feet tall, is still my mocha-baby, and always will be. Keagan started something very special in our family and showed us that we could very much love a child who was not biologically ours. Keagan is a legend in our family, and the leader of the pack!

Keagan-boy, you're such a joy,
At least until last week;
Now you are so crazy,
Well, you certainly are not meek!

You scream like a dinosaur,
Throw toys and tantrums too.
I have been truly wondering,

What on earth has gotten into you?

You love to be naked,
And it doesn't matter where.
In the house or in the yard,
There goes the underwear.

I've actually heard about this time,
It's called the terrible two's.
Parents who've been through it,
Say I should prepare to lose!

So, we have a plan, young man,
To get you through this mess.
We've talked to God about it,
And He knows you the best.

We'll love you through the bad days,
And cherish the good.
We'll praise you and lift you up,
When you do the things you should.

We'll pray to God for wisdom
When we want to pull our hair.
We'll enjoy those little tiny breaks
When you're in the time-out chair.

Soon when you're older,
We'll forget about these struggles.
We'll only remember all the songs,
The kisses and the snuggles

Chapter 8

Shea-Baby

I was busy being a momma to three children now, and things were humming along quite smoothly. We were not actively pursuing another adoption, but we knew we would adopt again. Keagan's adoption had been an amazing journey. Once again, we learned to rely on God's timing and not our own. And God decided it was time to move again.

It all began with a dream. It wasn't the first time God had spoken to me or showed me His plans through a dream, but it was the most memorable.

In my dream, Dale and I were in an office. As I looked out the window, I could see skyscrapers, which made me realize that we were in a large city. I looked down into a cradle and saw a milk chocolate baby with a huge, puffy head of hair and big, inquisitive eyes. A social worker was standing near us, and she began telling us that we did **not** have to take this baby girl home, that we were under no obligation with so many "unknowns."

When I woke from this dream, I knew it was important. It wasn't just an ordinary dream. I knew it was something God was preparing for me, and I was **excited**! I grabbed my prayer journal and quickly wrote down every detail I could remember, then I woke up Dale to tell him that I was convinced we had a baby girl on the way. The only part that intimidated me at all was the "unknowns." But seriously, doesn't every child come with unknowns? But I guess some unknowns are bigger than others.

Exactly one week later, we got the call. We were in our downstairs family room, watching the Olympic qualifying events. The call came from a caseworker I did not know; she had gotten my name and phone number from our adoption attorney. She informed us that she had a baby she was trying to place, but there were "unknowns."

"Where is this baby?" I asked.

"She's in Chicago."

A big city! The picture of those skyscrapers in my dream flashed through my mind, as did the image of the little girl.

"So, is this a girl?"

"Yes."

Um... is she African American, with lots of hair?"

Again, a "Yes."

"So, tell me; what's this little girl's challenge?" I asked.
Sounding surprised, she said, "Did we already call you?"

I laughed and told her that no one had previously called me, but I already knew this little cherub was my daughter. I just needed to know what we were facing.

This tiny baby was struggling. She had been born to a momma who had a significant crack cocaine addiction and had been working the streets to support her habit. This baby was the eighth child to which she had given birth, but the state of Illinois had stepped in and removed all of the other children from her care. They were waiting to take this baby as well, unless she made an adoption plan privately. So, momma, whose name was Terrie, had decided that making an adoption plan for her baby might be the only way to keep in touch with her child and have regular updates and, maybe, visits.

No sooner had we agreed to adopt this sweet baby than the hospital notified us that momma Terrie had pulled out her IVs and fled, leaving the baby behind. Apparently, she was facing some legal charges that she wanted to avoid. She left the baby at the hospital but had not signed the parental surrenders that would make it legal for us to adopt her.

We chose to take custody of the baby, understanding that it was an "at-risk" placement, as momma could change her mind and refuse to sign parental surrenders. Dale and I made the three-and-a-half-hour drive to Chicago to meet this princess that we decided to name Bronwyn Shea. She had been placed in a temporary foster home just outside of Chicago. The family caring for her were wonderful people who had photos of every baby they had ever cared for on their living room walls. It was impressive and beautiful!

Bronwyn, or "Shea baby," as we began to call her, was a sick young lady. She was suffering from severe withdrawals from her addiction to momma's crack cocaine. In addition, she had contracted chlamydia, which is a sexually transmitted disease passed from momma to baby through the birth canal. In babies, it generally settles in their lungs, so that was another battle we were fighting. She worried us, as she was slower to develop than most babies, took quite a while to smile, and didn't respond to things like most babies. But her "unknowns" did not keep us from loving her, from giving her every fighting chance we could. She was an adorable little chubster, and all of the other kids spoiled her even more than Dale and I did.

As an infant, Bronwyn would go through an ugly withdrawal episode about every hour. It involved hyperventilating and shaking and would last about eight to ten minutes. We would just hold her or stroke her face to comfort her through the episodes. We were told they would become less frequent and less severe over time, and within six months, they should be done. There could, however, be lasting effects from the addiction, such as developmental delays and mental impairment.

One afternoon, our Pastor Jim happened to stop by to visit at the exact time Bronwyn began having a withdrawal episode. He was horrified and prepared to call an ambulance. We explained to him what was happening in Bronwyn's little body, and he was even more appalled. He responded, "Get your hands on that sweet babe and pray these away!" I am truly not sure why we hadn't thought of that. We had prayed for her but not specifically when she needed it the most, so that is what we started to do. Every time Bronwyn had a withdrawal episode, our family gathered around her and prayed it away. Within a month, her withdrawals were completely gone, and so was her chlamydia. Jesus healed my baby girl!

As we were caring for Bronwyn and loving her more every day, her birth mother had finally been located and arrested. She was sentenced to three years at a prison not too far from our home. She, however, refused to sign the parental surrenders. Our attorney said we could still proceed with the adoption, but we would have to prove to the court that Bronwyn's birth parents were unable to provide for her care, which would be expensive and challenging. And it would mean taking her rights, instead of her surrendering them, which didn't feel ok with us. We decided to meet with her.

I had been to a prison visitation before, but Dale had not, so this was an entirely new experience for him. Terrie was a very sweet lady. Her speech was slurred, and often she did not make sense in her statements. Our visit ended up being a friendship that I cherish to this day. We visited her many times and exchanged letters even more often. I was able to share Christ with her, and I was able to explain to her that we would parent Bronwyn, but still allow Bronwyn to know who she was and where she came from. Nothing would be kept from her, and Terrie would remain a part of our lives, even after the adoption was finalized. One thing that upset her is that we had changed Bronwyn's name. She wanted us to keep the name she gave her, which was Justice Unique Eunice Allison Baker. She wanted Bronwyn to be called Justice. God showed me that this woman was mourning the loss of her other children and just needed reassurance that we were not going to adopt her child and then disappear from her life. We needed to respect her enough to consider her feelings and desires. So, Bronwyn became the McKinney with the longest name. Bronwyn Shea Justice Unique Eunice Allison Baker McKinney. This made Terrie very happy!

Things began to change for Terrie. She became more and more open to Jesus. And then one day she told us she had accepted Him as her Savior! She also told us that she had peace about signing parental surrenders so that we could move forward with Bronwyn's adoption. Both of these events were miracles. And another miracle was that after Terrie accepted Christ, her speech began to clear. Her letters were more and more legible, and her sentences were now clear and easy to understand. I do believe that God began to heal Terrie and was blessing her as well as us. God is so good!

Back on the home front, Bronwyn grew and developed, but again just a bit behind schedule. She walked at eighteen months instead of twelve like the other children. She was slower to respond and often seemed dazed, especially when we were out somewhere that overwhelmed her. Very often, she would have "zone-outs" where she was blank and would not respond to anything, even pain. We often wondered if these were seizures. We took her to several neurologists, who said they would not treat her for seizures but would continue to monitor her. Her history predisposed her to delays, and they felt like that is what we were seeing.

And then came the biggest miracle of Bronwyn's story. At about the age of three, everything changed. Bronwyn came alive, and she began to talk! Her physical movement became more fluid and less forced. She **wanted** to learn everything she could; in fact, she sat beside Keagan and I and learned letters and sounds right along with us. By the time she was five, she was reading fluently, and by age six she was reading chapter books. Every single delay had disappeared, and now her little mind was making up for lost time. She started school two years ahead of schedule and ended up graduating two years early at the age of sixteen. She was a straight

"A" student at a very challenging private school, and a captain on the basketball team.

Bronwyn is a miracle. She is evidence of God's healing hand and the love and devotion of a family. She has made us all so proud; she enrolled in ministry school in Alabama and had the opportunity to share her testimony several times. She also toured the country with an interpretive dance team that ministered to people at Christian conferences and street festivals.

Never be afraid of "unknowns." My "unknown" is such a blessing to me. And trust God, who can and does heal. If He asks you to parent a child with "unknowns," He will equip you to parent that child, even if healing does not come. Trust in the Lord, and then let Him do His thing!

Brown is the color
Of my baby's skin.
Pink is the color
Of the clothes I dress her in.
Black is the color
Of her pretty, curly hair.
Blue is the color
Of the shoes she likes to wear.
Orange is the color
Of her precious Oscar cat.
Purple is the color
Of her favorite beach hat.
Green is the color
Of her set of toy keys.
Gold is the color
Of what she's worth to me!

Chapter 9

Baby Ivy

When Bronwyn was about four weeks old, our wonderful adoption attorney, Kirsten, called us again. She had an African American baby girl that was due any day, and she could not find a family for this cherub. She was local, and the costs were low, so we committed this opportunity to prayer.

Having baby girls that were just a few weeks apart would be a lot like having twins. This baby was not born with prenatal drug or alcohol exposure, so she would not experience the withdrawals and sicknesses that Bronwyn endured. The more we prayed, the more we thought this might be a really great experience. So, we got really brave, stepped out in faith, and told Kirsten that we would adopt this baby girl.

We decided to name her Ivy and began planning where to put her cradle and how many more baby girl clothes we would need. We chose not to tell anyone until she was already home with us, so people wouldn't think we had gone totally crazy. (This was back when we worried about things like that.)

Weeks went by with no word from Kirsten. After a quick call, we learned that another agency had been able to find a home for this baby girl. We were sad, and we were happy; our emotions were all over the place. I think this is where we first learned to ask God to open and close doors for our family. God knows each baby before they are born. He knows their names and who their families are. We don't ever want to be outside of God's will. Partially through this experience, we learned the beautiful art of asking God to open or close doors regarding the children He chooses to be a part of our family. In this situation, the door closed. It hurt, but it was okay. God closed the door, and our trust was fully in Him.

Close the door,
Open the door;
Push me on through.

I'm standing at the crossroads,
And I don't know what to do.

Left could be the best way,
Or maybe it's to the right.

I just can't stop thinking about it,
Every day and night.

Open my eyes,
Shut my mouth;
Make me lean on you.

Only You can help me
Find the path that's straight and true.

Chapter 10

Tobin

Dale and I were settling into being a family with four children. Things were going much smoother than we expected. I was homeschooling Brogan and Patrick, while Keagan and Bronwyn attended a small Christian preschool not far from our home. Everyone was happy and healthy. Dale and I were both working too much, but I hired a dear friend to help with the children while I worked. My mother had always cared for Brogan and Patrick when they were younger, but she was now caring for my sister's children. So, Carol, an exceptional friend to this very day, not only assisted in my grooming salon and cleaned my house, but now she also helped care for the kids. They loved her, and she treated them like her own. Carol was a Godsend.

One day, in March of 2002, I got a call from my adoption attorney, Kirsten. She was seeking a family for an African American baby girl who was due in May. This adoption situation was a little different, as this baby was to be born in either Mississippi or

Louisiana. The birth mom, Yvette,* was a professional woman who had found herself in a crisis pregnancy that she didn't want her friends and family to know of. She wanted a closed adoption. This was so different from the open adoptions that we had come to appreciate with Keagan and Bronwyn, but we hoped that maybe after some time, we could have contact with this
baby's birth mother.

Dale and I agreed to move forward with the adoption and named our new daughter Brenna Michele. Brenna was a name that appealed to both of us, and Michele had been my dear friend from high school. For some reason, right after we said yes, we both felt an urgency to tell our extended families. I know now that God was moving on our hearts because He knew we would need their support sooner than expected. So that very evening, we visited my parents and shared the news with them, and we later called Dale's parents to let them know. Both families were surprised, but not shocked; they knew how much our previous adoptions had blessed us.

Early the next day, on March 13, I headed to a homeschooling conference at a local church. As I was sitting in the (somewhat boring) meeting, one of my employees peeked her head in the door. I was immediately worried, thinking one of the children might be hurt or sick. As I sneaked out the side door, I sensed her excitement.

"Ann, you'll never guess what phone call Dale got!"

"Please tell me, quick!"

"Birth momma is in active labor and you need to head south right away!"

"Oh my…"

"Dale already started packing. Come. Hurry!"

By the time I got home, Dale had every child dressed and their bags packed, and they were waiting for me in their car seats. He had also made arrangements with his employer to take an emergency leave for a week. And so, we headed to Tallulah, Louisiana, to meet our new baby girl. We prayed that we would get there before she was born, but since it was a nine-and-a-half hour drive, it was doubtful. This was birth mom's third baby, and she wanted her to come quickly.

As we drove, and sang, and dreamed of this new family member, our attorney called to tell us that the baby was being born at a

61

hospital in Vicksburg, Mississippi. Since the baby was about eight weeks early, she might need to be transferred to a larger children's hospital, depending on how her lungs were developed. We drove, we prayed, we tried to sneak in a nap, but we were all too excited!

We arrived at the hospital in Vicksburg, tired but so excited to meet our new daughter.

The lady at the front desk smiled up at us.

"Hi, how can I help you?"

"We are Dale and Ann McKinney, and we are here to meet Yvette. She just had a baby girl, and we are the adoptive parents."

A long silence ensued as she scanned her monitor, and I could hardly keep from fidgeting.

"I'm sorry, Mr. and Mrs. McKinney, but we don't have anyone with that name who had a baby girl."

My stomach knotted.

"But- we just drove nine hours because she was in labor and was giving birth to a baby girl. I don't understand."

"You're sure about the mother's name?"
"Yes."

"Hmmm… well, okay, there is a Yvette who gave birth to a **boy**."

"Oh, my word! A boy?" I laughed, knowing that Dale had only grabbed baby girl clothing, and Brogan and Bronwyn cried, as they were so disappointed. They had been gloating the entire trip that this baby was a tie-breaker! The baby was still a tie-breaker, but in favor of the boys. We were now parents to three boys and two girls.

A nurse directed us to Yvette's recovery room, where we spent a few minutes getting to know this elegant, calm, and self-assured woman. She certainly did not look as though she just had a baby! She told us that the baby was having some struggles breathing, but she was sure he would be okay. She had a beautiful smile and was very soft-spoken yet reassuring. To this day, I wish we had spent more time with her and gotten to know her better. We did find out that she had successfully kept this pregnancy a secret. No one knew she had given birth, and she wanted it to stay that way. In fact, she was planning to head back to her home that evening.

Yvette signed nursery consents for us so that we could finally meet this new little member of our family. She also told us that his father's name was Thomas* and that if she had decided to parent, that is what she would have named him. But she gave us permission to choose a name that would "fit" our family.

The little guy was struggling. He was **so** tiny! He was born weighing four pounds, two ounces, which was a good size for only thirty-two weeks of gestation. But he just seemed so small compared to all my previous babies. His breaths were labored, and he seemed to be having some pain. He was on oxygen and had many other monitors attached, so we were not allowed to hold him. When I touched him or rubbed his face, it seemed to annoy him, and he tried to pull away. But he was so cute! He had the perfect shade of milk chocolate, with a small amount of soft fuzzy hair. He had very long fingers and toes.

We all gave him sweet kisses and prayed over him, and then we were asked to leave so the doctors could continue to run tests and monitor him closely. The staff at the hospital was very accommodating and showed us to a Ronald McDonald house, where we were able to stay close to the hospital for $10 per night. It was an inviting place and certainly pleasing to our budget since we thought we had a few months to save funds for this trip.

I had a restless night—thoughts of that sweet, nameless boy kept tumbling through my mind. I was worried, but also excited. I only slept a few hours and woke to the rising sun and a firm *knock-knock* on our door. I hurried to open it. The house manager was standing there, a concerned look on her face.

"I'm sorry to disturb you, Mrs. McKinney, but they called from the hospital and said your baby has gotten worse overnight. They had to airlift him to the Children's Hospital in Jackson, Mississippi. They said he needed a ventilator."

"Oh, no! Why didn't they let us know sooner? Our poor baby."

We were devastated and shocked that no one had let us know before now. Our sweet baby had been airlifted to another state, all alone, and no one had told us. This was crazy. This, we later found out, was because we had no legal rights to the baby at this time. The birth mom could not sign surrenders until day five in Mississippi, so she was still his legal guardian at this point. Each state has different adoption/nursery laws, and Mississippi was very different than what we were used to in Illinois.

We quickly packed up and made the two-hour drive to Jackson. Arriving at the NICU, we were again told we had no legal right to see the baby, have information about his health, or even know if he was alive. We called both attorneys involved in our case, but neither one could be of any help. It was a Saturday, and the hospital attorneys would not be back in their offices until Monday morning.

We spoke with an emergency attorney who represented the hospital, and she reassured us that our baby was alive and being cared for. Still, she could not and would not divulge any further information until parental surrenders were on her desk. All three attorneys involved in our case advised us to go home. They let us know that on day five—after birth mom signed her parental surrenders—we would have full access to all information about our son. We would then be able to see him and speak directly to the doctors who were caring for him.

We were so sad. So depressed. This was not at all how we thought this trip would go. No one spoke for hours on the drive home. We talked about staying, but we knew this could mean weeks or months of hospitalization for our baby, and we could not afford to miss that much work. We now had no idea how much this hospitalization would cost us or how many more attorneys' bills we would be receiving.

Dale had the idea of finding something fun to do to cheer us all up. He found a family amusement center, and it was full of games, jumping activities, an arcade, and more. It was so good to see the kids all smiling again!

We ate pizza and discussed what we were going to name our little peanut. After much debate, we decided on Solomon Exod. Solomon, after the wisest man in the Bible, and Exod, after a friend we met on a Haiti mission trip. Once the pizza was gone, Dale and I each took two kids in separate directions to play a few more games.

We had just started a game when I heard Brogan scream, and she ran to me, covering her eyes and shrieking. After I got her calmed down enough to talk, she told me that a man had been standing outside the glass emergency exit doors and had motioned for her to come closer. She stood still in her tracks. When he realized she wasn't coming closer, he pulled down his pants and began to fondle himself in front of her. Dale ran for the doors, hoping to catch this pervert, while I carried Brogan and Bronwyn to the front counter to alert the manager. We were told this was not the first time this man had visited the amusement center, but he had not been caught. They were terribly sorry. And that was it. We left, even more depressed than we already had been.

The only thing that sustained me for the next few days was knowing that God was watching over little Solomon and that he was still alive. The days moved so slowly until, finally, day five arrived, and Yolanda went to court. The moment the surrenders were signed, the Mississippi attorney faxed them to the hospital and gave me the green light to call the NICU. My fingers trembled as I dialed and waited.

"Hello, how may I help you?"

"This is Ann McKinney, and I'd like to speak to Dr. Melton"*

"One moment, please."

I couldn't believe I would finally get the details about my baby Solomon.

"Hello, Mrs. McKinney, this is Dr. Melton. I am so happy to hear from you."

"Please tell me, how is baby Solomon doing? I have waited so long and I want every detail!"

"Well, Mrs. McKinney, he is in stable condition. You may not know this, but his left lung collapsed and that's why they airlifted him to Jackson. We placed a chest tube, and he is still on the ventilator to allow his lungs to heal and grow. That's really the only thing we're waiting on right now."

"I am so relieved to hear that! Are there any other complications?"

"He does have an umbilical and inguinal hernia that will need repairing after he is older and a bit healthier."

"Thank you, Dr. Melton, for taking such good care of our baby. It's been so difficult to not be with him and not know what was really going on!"

"Listen, I'm happy we could take care of him! And we're also very glad to hear that baby Solomon has a family who already loves him and wants to take him home. We have far too many babies where that is not the case. Please feel free to call as often as you wish."

"Thank you, doctor, I surely will!"

And call I did! I called at least three times daily as we waited until Solomon was strong enough to be released from the hospital. My heart ached because I wanted to be there with him, but we could not find a way to make that happen. We knew this adoption was going to be much more expensive than we had anticipated, and neither Dale nor I could afford to miss much more work. So, we let Solomon rest and heal in God's hands.

Sometime over the course of Solomon's hospital stay, we all realized that we didn't like the name, Solomon. It just didn't fit our little guy. We spent a night of family devotion time discussing a new name for him. Since all four of our children had Irish names, we decided another Irish name was in order. So, Solomon Exod became Tobin Liam. Toby! Or Toby Li, as he became known. My preferred nickname for him was Little Tiny Toby Li.

After twenty-four days in the NICU, we finally got notice that Toby was ready to come home. He was to be released on Easter Sunday. What a special day for us to bring home our newest McKinney! Dale and I made arrangements for the grandparents to care for Brogan, Patrick, Keagan, and Bronwyn, and off we went to Mississippi. It was such a beautiful blessing to spend some time together, and I still have very fond memories of that long car ride with my sweetheart. We listened to lots of great music and had wonderful conversations on that drive! I love my family, but I missed my alone time with my husband.

The next morning, we stood looking at our beautiful son through the NICU incubator. We were surprised that Toby had not grown at all. In fact, he had lost weight and now weighed three pounds, eight ounces, but he was breathing calmly and was bright eyed and interested in his world. He was so cute! We rocked him and snuggled him, with plans to take him home with us the next day.

There were lots of feeding and care instructions to review before he would be released to us. Seeing so many sick babies in the NICU broke my heart, and my heart broke even more when the nurses told us that many of them either didn't have a family or else their families were not interested in visiting them. Dale and I quietly said a prayer for each one, especially for a little girl who seemed extra irritated.

Taking Toby home that day was so amazing. We had waited almost a month for this day. We loaded him into his car seat and packed our car with all of his feeding supplies, binders full of instructions, and health records. Toby slept most of the way home, and we only stopped a few times to feed him and get gas. The kids were over the moon excited to meet him. He was met with love at the front door and was quite spoiled for most of his infancy.

About two weeks after Toby came home, we got a disturbing call from our adoption attorney. The hospital had sent her a letter stating that Toby had been diagnosed with a blood disorder at birth. She faxed it to me, and as I skimmed over the document, my eyes stopped at the words, "Sickle Cell Disease." Now, in order to tell this story correctly, I need you to fully understand how God prepared me to receive this very letter on this very day. Here is some history on God's providence.

When I was in eighth grade, I had a science teacher named Mrs. Rayhill. She required all her students to do a research report on a disease. I chose to do my report on sickle cell disease. She tried her best to discourage me, reminding me that this was an African

American disease that would never affect my family or me. She thought it made more sense for me to learn about a disease that might one day affect my family. But I stood my ground, and I learned everything I could about this awful, painful, debilitating form of anemia.

It blows my mind to think that when I was a fourteen-year-old girl, not even thinking about motherhood, God was already preparing me to be a mother to little Toby. And even more crazy was that God brought these memories to my mind, and I truly could recall almost every detail I had learned about this disease.

Because of my previous knowledge of sickle cell disease, Toby's diagnosis did not terrify me. It made me sad because I fully understood the struggles and pain he would face in his life, but it did not make me change my mind or treat Toby differently. My doctor's office confirmed the diagnosis with a few blood tests and referred us to the St. Jude Midwest Affiliate clinic in Peoria, IL, which was about ninety miles from our home. This clinic—and Dr. Kay Saving and her staff—became almost like family to me, and their love and care for my son actually charted the course for my family's future. But I'm getting ahead of myself here.

In the meantime, my attorney was not a happy woman. The dates on the blood tests performed in Mississippi were just a few days after Toby's birth. The hospital knew Toby had a diagnosis of sickle cell disease when we brought him home—and all of the times we spoke on the phone—but not a single doctor or nurse had ever mentioned it to us. This was pretty significant medical news. My attorney made a few complaint calls to the hospital, and magically, our astronomical hospital bill disappeared!

To this day, we have never received a bill for Toby's hospital stay. Praise God! God had protected Toby and healed him of lung collapse, had brought him home to us safely, and had now eliminated the bill that could very well have bankrupted our family. We were doing the happy dance for days.

Toby's adoption ended up being one of our most complicated ones ever, and it was probably one of the most challenging adoptions our attorney ever completed. Toby's birth mom was separated but still legally married when she became pregnant. The biological father, who was never found or named, was not her husband. Toby had both a biological father and a legal father, Yolanda's ex-husband. Because Yolanda and her now ex-husband had been married at the time Toby was conceived, he had legal parental rights to Toby, and those had to be terminated. The problem was that he was in the military. The challenge of tracking him down when he was deployed overseas was nearly insurmountable, and the Soldiers and Sailors Act made it impossible to serve him termination documents when he was out of the country.

It took us six years to complete Toby's adoption, and sixteen years to receive a corrected birth certificate with Dale and I listed as his parents. I am glad I am not easily stressed, or this adoption would have taken a toll on me.

Toby is smart, handsome, very athletic, and gifted with anything mechanical. He battles sickle cell disease every single day, and I hurt for him when he wakes up with back and leg pain. He has had many pain crises that have required transfusions, and he has sickle damage to his lungs and kidneys. But he is happy and upbeat; he does not let this struggle steal his joy. Most recently, he has been contacted by his birth mother and siblings. Their conversations have been good and productive, and we welcome them back into our lives. My prayer is that, eventually, he will be able to meet them and learn more about this mother who gave him his life and his heritage. Toby is a treasure!

And so here we were, a family with five children. One with an on-going medical disease, and all of them busy, active, and a wee bit challenging in their own ways. And this was just the beginning.

Little Tiny Toby Li,
When I see you, what do I see?
Fuzzy black hair and mocha skin,
A round little belly and legs so thin.
Beady eyes of darkest black,
Pouty lips that hungrily smack.
A past so uncertain,
A future so bright;
Oh, Toby Li, you're a beautiful sight!

Chapter 11

Timothy

My babies were growing up! Brogan was seven, Patrick was six, Keagan was three, Bronwyn was almost two, and Toby was still a baby. Life was busy, but good. Dale was working as a paramedic, and I was still grooming pets in my salon. We had made one huge change to my business: We moved it home.

In our back yard, we had previously turned our garage into a kennel. Now, we added on to it and built a grooming salon in the front of the kennel. Every day, I homeschooled Brogan and Patrick in a school area in my salon, and Carol cared for Keagan, Bronwyn, and Toby in the house. I got to eat lunch with them every day, and at the end of each day they came out to my salon to help me clean up and care for the dogs we were boarding. I loved it!

I had a dear friend named Seanna, whom I had met at church. Seanna and I did a lot of things together, and she also helped me with my children and business. One day, she called to ask me a favor. She had met a woman named Jade,* who had been one of the largest drug dealers in our area and also very involved with the occult and witchcraft. She had been a very rough lady, but my dear Seanna had befriended her, shared God's love with her, and showed her a better way to get through life. Jade had accepted Christ and was now a sister!

Seanna wanted to take Jade to a Christian women's conference in Colorado, but Jade did not have anyone to care for her three-year-old son, Timmy, while she was gone. Seanna volunteered me. I was apprehensive, as this little guy did not know me, and I did not know him. But I was very excited to help Jade grow deeper in her relationship with Christ, so I agreed to babysit Timmy for the weekend.

Timmy was adorable. He was bi-racial like my Keagan, so he was a beautiful mocha shade. He had braids in his hair and sweet, pouty lips. He didn't speak much but was not at all afraid to come to my home. He and Keagan became best friends almost immediately, and they were never far from each other from day one.

Timmy was very afraid to be alone with an adult, which made me wonder whether he had been abused at some point in his life. We made a point never to be alone with him, as we didn't want to cause him any anxiety or concern.

Timmy was just learning about potty training, so he and Keagan spent a lot of time trying to figure out the whole peeing-in-the-toilet thing. One of my tricks for boys was to put Cheerios in the toilet and let the boys aim and try to hit them. Potty training and target practice at the same time! One of my fondest memories is of these two boys lined up with their little brown behinds facing the door, trying to hit those Cheerios!

We loved Timmy right away. Dale and I took many walks that weekend; I loaded Keagan, Timmy, and Bronwyn in the wagon, while Dale pushed Toby in his stroller.

The weekend flew by, and we had to find a way to let Timmy go back home. I was hoping we could offer to babysit him more often to give his momma a break and also spend more time with him.

Sunday evening came and went, but no one returned to claim little Timmy. Another week went by, and no one came or even called to let us know what was going on. Dale and I questioned if we should contact DCFS, but we didn't want him taken from us, so we just kept on caring for him and waiting. After two weeks, Jade called to let us know she was struggling. She asked if we could keep him a bit longer. We agreed and committed to praying for her every day.

We ended up caring for Timmy most of the summer. It was wonderful! Having another little boy to care for was not hard. Timmy was a sweet boy and very obedient. He finally caught on to toilet training, and he, Keagan, and Bronwyn were all done with diapers at the same time. I was quite proud of this accomplishment! We hoped that Jade would ask us to care for Timmy permanently, but we kept that desire in our hearts, as this was unchartered territory. This momma wanted to parent her son but was just having difficulty doing it.

Jade returned to claim Timmy at the end of summer. He cried. Keagan and Bronwyn cried. Toby even cried a bit, although I'm not sure he understood why he was crying. Dale and I cried, but we waited until Timmy left. We prayed that God would protect Timmy, as he was exposed to so many ugly things in his inner-city home environment. We had to remind ourselves that God loved Timmy more than we did.

We saw Timmy occasionally over the next few years, and he came to stay for the weekend now and then. We wanted to keep him more often, but again, we felt God calling us to be there for Jade only when she needed us. We reached out to her other children, twins named Michael and Radiance, as well. They were much older than Timmy but needed some stability and love as well.

I fondly remember the time I found out they were having a birthday, but Jade did not have money to get them a cake. So, I spent the day making birthday cakes that looked like pizzas! It was a lot of fun. Dale and I "adopted" Jade's family, and every year we made sure to have money in our budget to provide a happy Christmas for them.

When Timmy was in fifth grade, Jade called us again.

"Ann?? This is Jade, Timmy's mom."

"Hi, Jade, it's so good to hear from you! How's Timmy? How are you?"

"Well, I'm in a bit of a rough spot, and I was hoping you could help me out."

"Sure, tell me what's going on."

"I'm going to have to move and I'm not sure where to; can Timmy stay with you until I get settled somewhere?"

"Dale and I would be happy to help you out with Timmy. You know how we love that boy."

Jade agreed to give us temporary legal custody of Timmy so that we could enroll him in school and care for his medical needs. We were excited, Timmy was back in the house!

Timmy came to us with a backpack full of toy wrestling guys and a few pairs of clothes. He needed more clothing, a winter coat, and some school supplies. A quick post on Facebook, and those needs were met almost immediately by my generous band of friends.

We got Timmy set up for school, and I met with his teacher. Timmy needed a lot of help, as he was behind in his schoolwork, but Dale and I spent time with him each night, trying to get him working at grade level. We loved this time with Timmy. He was one of the sweetest, kindest boys I know. Timmy and Keagan's friendship deepened, and now they could actually tell people they were brothers! Well, sort of. They already looked so much alike that people thought they were twins.

It didn't last too long. Jade got back on her feet, and Timmy's father came back into the picture. He established himself as head of the household, and they took Timmy back home with them. We were sad to lose him again, but happy that he was going to experience life in a real family setting, with both his mom and dad there to care for him. We continued our relationship with Timmy. He was here almost every weekend to stay with Keagan, but we felt him drifting. The call of the world was enticing, and Timmy was exposed to it much more than my children were. He had drifted a bit more each time we saw him, which made us pray even harder.

When Timmy was in high school, he called me very early one morning. He was crying.
"Ann, I just came downstairs, and... and..."
"What's wrong, Timmy?"
"My mom is sick. I think she might be dead!"!"

"What? Oh, Timmy, I hope you are wrong. Are you alone?"

"No, my dad is here and he's trying to revive her."
"Did someone call the EMT's?"
"Yeah, they're on the way."

"I'm praying right now, Timmy. I'll wake up Dale and Keagan, and they'll be right over."

When Dale and Keagan arrived at Timmy's house, the police were already there, and there were people everywhere. Jade had been dead for some time, so they were waiting on the coroner. Jade's children and family members were hysterical, and Dale did his best to keep them calm and help in any way he could.

Poor, sweet Timmy. All he could think of were the times he disrespected his mother and disobeyed her. Dale encouraged him to remember the good times and not allow Satan to fill his mind with bad memories. We were so thankful that we could be there for Timmy, and even more thankful that he wanted us there.

Just months after Jade died, Timmy's father left him and moved in with another woman. Once again, Timmy had nowhere to live. We offered him a room with us, but he had reached the point in his life where he didn't like rules such as curfews or limits on social activities. He elected to move in with an uncle, which made us all a bit sad, but we tried to understand. He and Keagan still spent lots of time together, and he was at our home frequently. He was in our prayers constantly.

I am so crazy proud of the man Timmy has become. He grew up with a very distorted idea of what a family is, but he is doing his best to make sure his nieces and nephews are cared for and loved. He is working full-time and makes sure he always has money from each paycheck to take his niece and nephews out to lunch or buy them school supplies or clothes. He visits often, and every single time I see him, he hugs me and lets me know that he loves me. He has a heart of gold, and he will be a wonderful husband and daddy someday.

Timmy was never legally mine, but in my heart, he has always been my son. I love him just as much as I love the rest of my crew. He won me over the first day I met him. I consider it an honor that his mother chose me to help her in her times of crises, and I will always care and look out for Timmy as if he were my own. I love you, Tim-man. Your momma would be so proud!

Oh, my boys, please settle down!
You're bouncing my whole house around!
Did you eat too many sweets today?
How much chocolate did you say?
You need to go run a mile or two,
A thousand jumping jacks will do.
Even when you sit, you're twitching;
It's like a bug bite's got you itching.
Oh well, at least you are not boring,
But I cannot wait to hear you snoring!

Chapter 12

Rory and Ronan: Our first set of twins!

When little Toby turned four, Dale and I felt God calling us to adopt another child. The more we prayed over our family, the stronger this feeling got. We called Kirsten, our attorney, and asked her to add us to her list of waiting families. We didn't wait long.

Kirsten called us about a birth mom who was battling preterm labor with twin boys. She was already a single parent to two sons and could not fathom the idea of parenting two more sons alone. She thought she had plenty of time to make the decision and find a family, until her labor began early. At that point, medication was holding off her labor, but the adoptive family needed to be prepared to adopt preemie sons if the medication was not successful. The birth mom was referred to Kirsten and asked to see profiles of families interested in adopting her fraternal twin sons. She was specifically seeking families who were either transracial or who had children of African American heritage.

We already had an adoption profile on file with Kirsten, and after reviewing many files, the birth mother, whose name was Tae,*, asked to meet us. The Living Alternatives Crisis Pregnancy Center in Champaign, which was about an hour from us, would facilitate the adoption. We met with Tae a few days later at the Center.

Tae was a very tall, beautiful young woman, but she seemed so ashamed and depressed. Broken-spirited is how I would describe her. We were able to break the ice and get a few smiles from her, but it was a struggle. She told us she could not parent these babies and that their father was in prison, so he could not do so, either. The babies were to be delivered by C-section on April 17, 2006, if they could stay put until then. She had several other families to meet and said she would decide by the end of the week.

We prayed on the way home. "Lord, open the doors or close them! You know the path for our family. We would **love** to parent twins, but we also don't ever want to be outside of Your will!"

And then we went home, and we waited. Dale was much better at waiting than I was. I tried to busy myself.

88

By this point in our lives, our situation had changed drastically. Right after Toby was born, Dale was accepted into the SIU Physician Assistant program. This was a program to which he had applied for many years and was finally accepted! This meant huge changes for our family. Dale went to school four hours from home. He lived in a small rental house Monday through Friday and came home on weekends. It also meant that we no longer had his income, and still had to finance two households. I doubled my grooming and boarding hours, and with the help of all of our extended family and friends, we made it work.

Dale and I had agreed that when he graduated, I would retire and become a full-time mom. This is something I had never wanted until Toby came along, but more and more, I felt God calling me to homeschool my children and be with them every day.

After Dale graduated from SIU's PA program, he accepted a job that paid four times more than he had ever made in his life. We found a buyer for our home and my business and moved to a farm in the country. We had every animal imaginable and truly lived that homeschooling farm life. On the farm, keeping myself busy was easy. There were chickens to feed, hay to stack, horses to ride, fences to repair, poop to scoop, and always a child who wanted to play hide and seek in the hay loft. It was a great time in our lives!

I was in the barn milking my favorite goat, Helen, when Kirsten called. Tae had chosen **us** to parent her babies. Here we go again, this time with **twins**! I was so excited I accidentally dumped the entire pail of goat milk as I ran to the house to tell Dale and the kids.

Tae fought preterm labor for the next few months. While Dale and the kids attended a Superbowl party, I worked on washing, folding, and organizing baby clothes, as I was sure the babies were coming. I was frantic that their birth was imminent, but the days came and went with no birth. Tae was great at keeping me updated on their health. One twin was growing and thriving while the other twin's growth had stalled, so the doctors were concerned.

The days and weeks passed slowly, and the babies continued to stay put. This was good. The scheduled C-section date was quickly approaching, and we were so excited. We made arrangements for Grandma Marcia to babysit the kids while Dale and I headed to Champaign to be with Tae for the birth of our babies. We could not wait to meet them!

Tae had requested her sister be with her for the delivery, so we waited in the labor and delivery waiting room with our facilitator from the pregnancy, Greta, and Tae's mother, Helen. Both were very sweet ladies, and both were excited for us. Hours went by with no word—literally nothing. Everyone began to feel that there was a problem. Greta feared Tae had changed her mind and had chosen to parent the babies.

I couldn't sit anymore; it was making me crazy. I walked toward the nursery to see if I could catch a glimpse of the babies, and there they were: two incubators, with Tae's last name on them. One twin was husky, with a dark skin tone and coarse hair, while the other twin was smaller, with shorter hair and a reddish skin tone. I was drawn to the smaller twin, so my attention focused on him.

I watched as he struggled to move. He was swaddled in a blanket, and I could tell he was trying to free his arms. After he finally managed to break one arm free, he stuck it out of the blanket and kind of waved at me! I remember sucking in my breath, hard, as I realized that he had only two fingers on that sweet hand. A nurse walked over and removed his blanket, and several nurses and interns examined him. I got a good look at this sweet babe and discovered that he had short arms, with two fingers on one hand and a little, paddle-type webbed hand on the other. It didn't appear that he could bend his elbows. He was very calm, allowing the nurses to move him all around as they verified that there were no other anomalies.

Hours later, with still no word from Tae, we asked her mother if we should stay or head home. Again, we thought she must have decided to parent the twins since we had not heard a peep from her. Our original plan was to be with the babies as soon as they were born. It had now been about four hours.

Her mother went to talk to her and came back to tell us that she wanted to see us. We followed Helen to Trish's room where she was holding both babies.

She smiled up at us. "Aren't they sweet?"

Then the smile dropped from her face. "The doctor told me they both have a hole in their heart. It's something that will probably take care of itself as they grow, but if not, they'll have to have surgery to fix it. Their daddy had the same problem when he was little, and he had to have the surgery."

Tae also told us about the smallest twin's arms and showed them to us. The other twin did not have limb differences but was very agitated and fussy. She also told us that she thought she still wanted us to adopt them but was struggling with this decision.

Our facilitator from the pregnancy center, Greta, was a wonderful source of peace for all of us, as she spoke only positive words and loved on all of us. She took many photos of Tae and both babies and encouraged her to take her time in making such a huge decision. Dale and I decided to head home and let God work out this situation. But secretly, my heart was already mourning the potential loss of the boys.

Later that evening, we had still not gotten a phone call or message from Tae, so I called her room to see if we could bring the other children to the hospital to see the babies. Even if they were not going to be part of our family, we still wanted the kids to see these babies for which we had been praying. My parents wanted to go with us.

93

At the hospital, Tae was holding the larger twin, with the smaller one in his bassinet beside her.

I picked up the little guy, and we sat close to Tae.

"Listen," she said. "I really do want you to be the parents to my little boys, but..." She paused, and tears filled her eyes. "But I just want to spend as much time with them as I can before you take them home."

My heart ached at the pain in her voice. "But of course, Tae! We understand." I placed the smaller twin in her arms beside his brother, and we walked out into the corridor to give her some time with her two precious babies.

After some time, we reentered the room and resumed the conversation.

"Tae, since we're planning on bringing these boys into our family, we have decided on their names already. We've given all our other children Irish names, and we'd like to continue that tradition, so we decided on Ronan and Rory. What do you think?"
She looked at us, glanced down at the babies in her arms, then gazed thoughtfully out the window. "Ronan and Rory. Hmm... Well,

they're for sure not Irish, but I do like those names!" She smiled, and I breathed a sigh of relief. With thankful hearts, we helped her fill out the application to request their birth certificates and social security cards.

We met a few more of her family members who came by to visit, and we got to snuggle all over little Rory, our first limb difference child. Tae allowed us to touch and talk to Ronan but would not let us take him from her. This was okay with us, although looking back, we should have recognized the turmoil in her heart.

Meeting with the orthopedic doctor at the hospital the next day was sobering. He examined Rory thoroughly and told us his concerns. First, there were many syndromes that could have produced the limb differences and heart defects Rory had. We would need to see a geneticist. And, truthfully, there was not much that could be done for Rory. There was no way to create an elbow, and the doctor felt that Rory would be very disabled, even to the point of needing help with everyday activities such as eating, dressing, and toileting.

As the doctor continued speaking, a conviction welled up inside of me; I was this baby's champion, and I would do anything and everything to empower this sweet little boy! He was stuck with me as a momma, and I was going to be there for him.

The babies were scheduled for discharge the following day. We knew there was an issue when our attorney told us to call her from the hospital. It seemed that Tae had still been struggling with making a decision. She now wanted to parent these babies, but she knew her support and resources were limited. This was a true crisis pregnancy/birth. She wanted more time to make her decision.

Kirsten had met with the judge who would be handling this adoption, and the judge agreed to grant her thirty days. So now we had a decision to make. We could take them home and love on them, but we had to understand that they could be going back to Tae on day thirty. Or, to protect our hearts, we could place them in a temporary foster care home until Tae made her decision. We elected to take them home.

Life with twins was crazy, but it became even crazier with the stress of not knowing whether we would have them for thirty days or forever. God sustained us and kept us busy enough that we didn't have much extra time to fret.

Rory was such a good baby. He rarely cried, loved to be snuggled, and was quite the little charmer. Some people were hesitant to approach him because of his hands, but his sweet smile quickly won them over.

Ronan, on the other hand... **oh my**. I don't think he ever slept more than thirty minutes. He did not like to be held or even touched. He was the most agitated, irritated baby I had ever been around, and he just screamed most of the time. I was exhausted after the first week, mostly from trying to soothe Ronan twenty-four hours a day.

Once, my sweet mother-in-law, Ginger, offered to come stay overnight so that I could get a solid night of rest. But the poor woman got violently ill at bedtime and had to head home, carrying a puke bucket. But I was thankful that she was able to help me out for a few hours.

I don't remember much of those first few weeks because I was so incredibly busy caring for the twins, trying to get Ronan to stop crying, homeschooling the kids through the chaos, and keeping the farm afloat. On day twenty-six, I went outside to sit on my porch and enjoy the fresh air. I needed a break, even if it was for just a few moments. My cell phone rang, and I noticed the call was from Kirsten. This phone call was probably the call that would decide the fate of our sweet babes. I was terrified to answer, but I knew I had to.

Yes, it was Kirsten. Tae would allow us to adopt Rory. She knew he needed special care, possible surgeries, and to see doctors that were not in this area. She felt she could not meet his needs and knew we could, but she wanted to parent Ronan. She was separating the twins. I could not believe it. This was an option we had not even realized she was considering. I was shocked, mad, and sad. God had put these babies in the womb together, and the thought of separating them broke my heart. But the choice was not mine.

I sat on the porch of my old farmhouse and cried big, ugly, alligator tears. I didn't even see my sister pull up. My sweet sister, Susan, attempted to console me and tried her best to remind me to trust God and to rejoice that we were chosen to parent Rory. I appreciated God sending her to me at that very time. It did help.

The following day was Sunday, and we took Ronan and Rory forward to be dedicated and prayed over. The entire congregation gathered and prayed over baby Ronan. There were a lot of tears and a lot of broken hearts. It was a very rough day.

The next day, Dale and Patrick loaded Ronan into his car seat, along with all of his belongings that I had packed. I kissed him one last time, and they drove away. And I cried some more. This time I snuggled Rory as I cried. He seemed to understand as he watched me with those big brown eyes. God, I'm totally trusting you on this. Please protect and bless baby Ronan! And just like that, he was gone. And then there was one.

But that one was so easy to fall in love with! I think that, out of all of my children, Rory was the most chill, the most easy-going, the happiest.

My doctor had made referrals for Rory to see a geneticist as well as for various therapy evaluations. The blood tests taken by the geneticist confirmed that there were no known syndromes matching Rory's condition.

We were very blessed to be able to enroll Rory in a program called Early Intervention, which provided therapy services for him in our home. We had an amazing occupational therapist, Miss Kimmie, whom Rory adored, and other therapists who came to our home each week to help Rory learn to use his hands and arms for simple daily tasks. The funny thing was that they always thought they had found the perfect way for Rory to do something, and then he would find his own way. From the beginning, he was very compliant but also very innovative. He knew what he wanted to do, and he found a way to do it.

When Rory was about a year old, I heard about a doctor in Baltimore who had been having success constructing an elbow in a child without one. I immediately contacted him and set up a consultation.

Rory and I flew to Baltimore many times over the course of several years for surgeries and follow-up appointments. His first surgery was to separate the webbed fingers on his longer arm. There were three fused fingers; however, the middle finger was all skin and no bone. The two outer fingers were solid. During surgery, they were able to separate those fingers, using skin from his groin as a graft. We had to lose the middle finger, but this doctor was able to move one of the remaining fingers around to give Rory a pincher grasp instead of the fingers being side by side. This was a vast improvement and gave Rory a grasp that he had not had previously.

The next surgery was to attempt to create an elbow on that same arm. This procedure was more difficult, primarily because the muscles and tendons in Rory's upper arm had never functioned and were severely atrophied. The surgery was not successful. It ended up being very painful to Rory. The doctor wanted to repeat it but admitted to us that it had a less than 20 percent chance of being successful. We opted to pass.

Rory grew and thrived. He never did require any surgery on his heart; the hole healed perfectly. His arms continued to be his only challenge. There were very few things he could not do, but having people stare at him and ask him about his arms was a big issue from early on. I am still, to this day, amazed at how cruel people can be and how ridiculous they can act when they see someone different. Yes, even adults.

Rory learned at an early age how to cope with this unwanted attention. He made up stories. If someone asked him what happened to his arms, he would say a lion attacked him, or that he was actually an alien. At first, I was upset at these stories he would tell, but then I relaxed. Rory needed to figure this out, and he was trying different ways to do that. Over time he learned to be more truthful, but secretly, I miss the fun stories!

Throughout the years we have attempted a few more surgeries, had him fitted for a prosthetic arm, and sought out more doctors. But in the end, Rory is Rory! As medical technology improves and new procedures become available, we will pursue them. But for now, he is content with how God made him. Personally, I love those sweet little fingers, and I often tell him how he won my heart at first glance when he waved at me that day in the incubator.

Rory is tall, almost six foot already. Tall, just like his birth momma. He is very handsome, he's a big flirt, and he always has a few girls calling. He does become discouraged about his arms at times, especially after someone stares at him. It still bothers him. But he knows that God made him, and that God doesn't make mistakes.

Rory is very spiritual, and I do believe God has big plans for him. The first moment my mother held him, she felt God telling her he was going to be in ministry, and he feels that call already. I do believe that people will look at Rory to see his differences, but Rory will use this as his platform to share Christ with them. The future is bright, Rory; I love you!

There's nothing like a kissy
That comes from a big sissy.
A brother is a friend
Whose love will never end.
Fight and argue as they might,
There's just nothing quite like
That special bond of love
That comes from God above,
That my children seem to share
As they pull each other's hair,
As they tattle on each other
And forever scream out, "Mother!"
I try to stop and think
How my life would surely stink,
If my house was really quiet
With no signs of a riot.
Thank you, God, for the pouts,
For the fights and the time-outs.
Help me smile instead of scream
And trade my stress for ice cream!

Chapter 13

MengYan

We had a really hard time with losing Ronan. We all felt like there was a giant hole left in our family, and we noticed that Rory, even as an infant, especially seemed to mourn his loss. Rory had never been without his brother from day one of conception, and now he was alone. While there was always someone ready to play with him or snuggle him, there was still a void.

When Rory was through his surgeries and on a predictable therapy schedule, we decided to fill that void by adopting again. We reached out to Kirsten, and she surprised us. She actually had many families on her waiting list for minority or special needs children. We rejoiced that people were finally becoming more open-minded about these precious children, but we weren't sure where that left us. We prayed that God would show us our next move, as we certainly did not feel that our family was complete.

After some internet searching, we discovered that China had, again, opened their adoption program to families with biological

104

children. The wait for a non-special-needs child was, on average, three to five years, but thousands of special needs children were ready and waiting to be adopted. We found an agency called WACAP and requested information about their international adoption program. When the packet came, we were excited to see that it contained a booklet of dozens of photos and bios from children who needed families. It was weird, almost like shopping for Christmas gifts in the JC Penney's catalog, only this was a catalog full of beautiful, orphaned children.

I went through the booklet first and took notes on each child in which I was interested. I noted their special need, age and sex, country of residence, and any grants or fee reductions applied to that child. The fees for international adoption were staggering, almost three times more expensive than for our domestic adoptions. I chose my top three children, which again felt so very weird. I kept my notes to myself and let Dale choose.

Dale chose his children of interest, we prayed, and then we compared notes. There were two children we had both chosen, so those were the children we prayed about. It was difficult to find a child who was in the right age range and had a special need that we felt confident we could manage. And then we talked to the kids, who were excited but apprehensive. The younger kids were baffled at how on earth we would learn to communicate with this child, and the older ones were intimidated by the amount of money we would have to save/raise. I think they all thought we would have to eat beans and rice for a year!

In the end, all of us settled on the same child. She was a sweet little Asian princess by the name of Chang MengYan, who was three years old. When Dale announced that MengYan had been chosen, little Bronwyn began to cry. She was upset because we did not choose the child that she wanted. We asked her to show us which child she wanted for her sister, and she pointed to the photo of MengYan! That was our first confirmation that this was our child. The second confirmation was when I asked Toby's St. Jude hematologist, Dr. Saving, to review MengYan's file. We needed to know that they could care for her at their facility. Dr. Saving assured us that they could successfully care for MengYan and encouraged us to go get our girl. That was all we needed to hear. We would find out how to navigate this new world of international adoption, and we would bring this sweet little toddler girl home!

We hit a lot of roadblocks right out of the gate. Our previous home study agency assured us they could complete an international home study for us, but we later found out they had never done this before. Also, the Hague Agreement, which regulated international adoptions, had just gone into effect, and no one knew how to meet the requirements for it. Our placing agency, WACAP, was able to lock MengYan's file so she was held for us but completing our home study was a nightmare. What should have taken us three months ended up taking over a year. Our caseworker would continue to make promises she could not keep and tell us information that was not correct. It was a year of torment and frustration. We had to ask for many extensions because our home study was not ready by the deadlines. Finally, our WACAP caseworker emailed us a template of exactly how to write our home study. That template (and a whole lot of nagging from me) is what got our home study caseworker to—finally—get our document completed.

In the meantime, we learned a lot more about MengYan. She had been abandoned as an infant in her home city and was found on the steps of the police department. They had transferred her to an orphanage, where she stayed until she was about sixteen months old. At this point, MengYan got very sick. She was dying, and they took her to a hospital for treatment. She was eventually diagnosed with beta-thalassemia major, often called Chinese/Mediterranean anemia. This was a big blow. Children with this disease produce defective red blood cells that are not capable of sustaining life. These children are required to have blood transfusions at least once a month and sometimes even more frequently.

China has a "survival of the fittest" philosophy, so the doctors caring for her elected not to pursue treatment. That statement is written in her adoption file; they were choosing to let her die. Heartbreaking! Can you even imagine this happening in the US? It's unthinkable, but it happens every day in China.

MengYan was placed in a bassinet and put into a storage closet, alone. In the dark. My heart breaks just writing this. An American woman happened to be there at the time and thought she heard the mewing of a kitten. She began to snoop around, opened the closet door, and found MengYan. This woman was Bonnie, who became MengYan's advocate. She convinced the hospital to release MengYan to her care, and then she placed her into an orphanage for medically fragile children. It was called Shepherd's Field Children's Village. Bonnie and Shepherd's Field together saved MengYan's life.

The staff at Shepherd's Field were not very familiar with thalassemia, but they did make sure MengYan had transfusions on a regular basis. Two different groups, Packages of Hope and ChangDe Kids both fundraised to pay for her transfusions and her care. I can never thank these people enough! Many other families donated for our girl and prayed for her health until a family could be found. Bonnie even wrote a book, *A Little Starfish,* to raise funds for MengYan. All of these things were happening while we were cluelessly working on that problematic home study. God was sustaining our girl through the hearts and actions of others while we were halfway across the world, praying for her. Beautiful!

Finally, our home study was complete, and our dossier was sent to China. Again, the Hague Program slowed the process down, but it still moved faster than the home study process. One thing that kept me sane through all of the waiting and stress was Brogan, my oldest daughter. She had begun courting Zachary, the son of my dear friend, Kimberly, and little by little, things got more serious. As

Zach prepared to leave for Army boot camp, they decided they couldn't live without each other. They became engaged, and we began to plan for a Christmas wedding. So exciting; I was gaining a son-in-law and a new daughter. Oh, how I hoped that little MengYan would be home in time to be the flower girl!

WACAP was very professional at walking us through the necessary steps, and finally, in September of 2009, we were invited by China to come and get MengYan. More blood, sweat, tears, and prayers had gone into this adoption than any before, so this was a blessed victory. Satan had worked hard to bring death to this child, and even harder to prevent us from being her parents, but he had been defeated, praise God! We began to pack.

My faithful friend Carol, as well as my parents, helped care for our kids as we headed out the door for our trip of a lifetime. I had always wanted to see China. Once I had even signed up for a short-term mission trip there, but it had been canceled. As I was growing up, one of my heroes was a missionary named Mary G, who served in China. I loved it when she returned to our church to share about her adventures in this fascinating country. Mary inspired me more than she will ever know, because she gave me a love for China before I ever stepped foot on Chinese soil. And now we were on our way. This was the great adventure!

After a fourteen-hour flight, we arrived in China. It smelled weird. It was hot and humid and oh, so smoggy. There were people everywhere. It reminded me of New York City, but even busier. The staff from Shepherd's Field met us at the gate and were so excited for us to meet MengYan. They had given her the English name of Emily and had called her that often to get her used to it. It was about an hour's drive to get to the facility, which was beautiful, and we were then shown to our comfortable and well-appointed room.

We had just finished settling in when there was a knock on the door. Dale opened it to find Jewel,* a Shepherd's Field staff member, standing there.

"I hope you're comfortable," she said. "I just want to tell you that MengYan has had a rough day and is very tired, and as late as it is, we thought it best for you to wait till morning to meet her."
Dale paused as I stepped up beside him. "Well, that's disappointing, but we do understand, don't we, Ann?"

My heart was broken, but what could I say? "Yes, of course."

Jewel smiled. "We would like for you to have dinner with us, though. That way, we'll have time to tell you more about her family and fill you in on some of her medical needs. See you in ten?"

We quickly spruced up for dinner and headed downstairs to the entrance, but just as we were leaving, here came an ayi (nanny) walking hand in hand with little MengYan! They had changed their minds and decided we could take her to dinner with us.

She was so cute, but her belly was unnaturally large and round. She had cute little piggy tails, and they had dressed her in an adorable outfit. She even had fuzzy pink tennis shoes, unlike any I had seen before. I knelt to talk to her, and she was quickly apprehensive. I pulled out some M&M's and all of a sudden, we became best friends. Oh, she loved chocolate, just like her momma! She avoided looking at or interacting with Dale, but we were told to expect this, and I knew he could win her over. She didn't want to be carried, partly because she wanted to be a big girl and partly because she was uncomfortable. Her belly was so swollen it hurt her to be lifted. So, together, we all walked down the road to a local restaurant.

We were in awe of how much this little child ate. She ate three times what I expected her to. We had a wonderful first meal in China, and our new daughter was precious. On the way back to the facility, we were invited to visit her foster home and meet some of the other children. We had come to know these children through photos and updates from the staff at Shepherds Field, so we were excited to finally meet them.

MengYan's best friend was a hilarious little girl named Margaret, also called NuiNui. She had a severe heart defect, but it didn't stop her, and she had a great time chasing Dale around the room. We were also blessed to meet Tiffany (MeiMei), Luke, Tristan (RDu), Ginger, and many others. They were all housed together in an exceptional home called the Samaritan House. All these children had severe special needs and were cared for lovingly by staff and ayis. We had the privilege of helping them all into bed and tucking them in for the night. It was a very special evening!

The following day we had nothing but time, so we spent the entire day getting to know MengYan. We learned that she loved to eat, loved to play with playdough, and loved any kind of crafts. But we also learned that she was very sick. She sweated profusely and could not walk far because her belly was so swollen and painful. From her medical records, we learned that her hemoglobin was generally between two and four. This was barely life-sustaining. Dale was very concerned with her belly, which was hard as a rock and painful. He was worried that she might have a Wilms tumor, or something similar.

MengYan was gradually warming up to Dale. It was funny, but she was intrigued by his goatee. She wasn't quite sure what to do with it, and she was even a bit afraid of it. Then, at one point, she reached out and pulled a hair from his chin. She looked at it, smelled it, and then tossed it over her shoulder, and then she was no longer afraid.

That evening we decided to keep MengYan in our bedroom. As soon as she realized that she was not going back with her friends, she threw an absolute fit. She yelled, screamed, kicked, tried to hit, and sobbed. And then she fell asleep. Our first full day as MengYan's parents was over, and it had been good. Things were going much smoother and easier than I had expected.

The next day we said goodbye to Meng's friends, the staff at Shepherd's Field, and her favorite ayi and headed to the airport. We flew to Hunan Province to go to court to officially adopt MengYan. Meng fussed a bit on the plane but was all smiles once we landed. We stayed in a nice hotel and had a wonderful guide who walked us through the process of exchanging money and preparing our court documents. She also showed us great places to shop and eat.

Our court process was very different from adopting a child in the US. We paid our fees, signed many papers, and had a short interview with a notary. Then we posed for photos, and it was all over; MengYan was now officially Emily MengYan McKinney. And now we needed to prepare for another flight. This time we were headed to Guangzhou to complete the immigration requirements for Meng's adoption. Very soon, she would be a US citizen.

Guangzhou was awesome! We stayed at a five-star hotel and met dozens of other adoptive families. There were so many things to see and do. But Meng began to get sick. Each day she had less energy and looked increasingly pale. We knew she probably needed a blood transfusion, and it was vital for her to have it before she flew home.

Our new guide, Mui,* helped us find a hospital; we visited three different ones before finding one that agreed to treat our daughter. This hospital was crowded and dirty, and I wasn't sure I wanted to have Meng treated here, but I also wasn't sure we had a choice!

Mui helped us explain that our daughter needed a blood transfusion, and we waited on the blood for several hours. When it finally came, it was a unit of warm, whole blood. This was very different than what I was used to in the US; I honestly think someone had just donated it! The nurse set up an IV for Meng and administered the blood over the course of the next hour. We sat with Meng in a room that resembled a theater. Almost every seat was occupied by someone getting an IV treatment of some sort. Meng seemed to perk up a bit after her transfusion and had a little more color in her cheeks, but we were still worried. She still did not have the stamina to walk much, and she still dripped sweat during any activity.

We made it through Meng's required medical exam and her citizenship ceremony, and at last, it was time to head home. We were so homesick! I don't think I have ever missed my children more. It was difficult to talk with them, as this was before cell phones and VPNs made communications easy. We were concerned about how Meng would handle the fourteen-hour flight home, but we knew she would be happy if she had food. So, we stocked up on her favorites: crackers, cookies, and those M&M's. We were so excited for everyone to meet her!

Our flight home was difficult. Meng was very uncomfortable; she cried out many times and didn't sleep at all. After a bit, her snacks didn't help much, and even the TV didn't make her happy. She continued to want to get up to go to the bathroom. After many trips down the long aisle of the plane, I realized she just wanted out of that seat.

We landed in Chicago in the early evening, collected our luggage, and began the three-and-a-half-hour drive home. Pulling up to the farm was so wonderful. I was so happy to see the kids, I cried! Toby, Bronwyn, and Rory fought over MengYan and wanted to carry her all over the house. It was already time for bed, so we made Meng a small bed in our room. She cried, kicked, screamed, and was terrified. It was Toby who came to our room and snuggled her to sleep. It was so sweet! Tomorrow was a big day of medical appointments, and she needed her rest.

The next day, I was exhausted, so Dale took Meng to the St. Jude Midwest Affiliate Clinic in Peoria, IL. We had been to this clinic numerous times with Toby, so the faces and facility were very familiar. We quickly learned how sick our little girl was. Her hemoglobin, despite the transfusion in China, was at three. She was in congestive heart failure, and that huge stomach? Well, that was the largest spleen on record to this day at OSF St. Francis Hospital. She was admitted to the hospital and spent three nights having tests and receiving blood transfusions. It took five transfusions to get her to a level with which the doctors were comfortable.

We met with a team of specialists and planned out the next few steps of Meng's care. Her spleen was so massive because it had been crunching up her red blood cells as fast as she got them. She was in congestive heart failure because she was given whole blood in China, instead of the packed red cells, which were all she needed. This had caused her to have a fluid overload. We learned that the transfusion should have also been given much more slowly. We concluded that we needed to start her on a hyper-transfusional schedule, which would keep her hemoglobin above nine, using donor blood. If we could keep her at this level, her body would stop making its own blood, and, hopefully, we could get her spleen to calm down. It would mean going to Peoria every seven to ten days for the entire day, but it's what we needed to do for our girl.

Every day, Meng got healthier and better adapted to our family. We could tell right away that she was incredibly smart. She learned English quickly, was soon able to write her name, and learning her colors and the alphabet were a breeze. At first, she was too weak to walk up the stairs, but with time, she mastered them. She eventually became strong enough to follow us to the barn and help with barn chores. Her transfusions were working, and we watched that belly shrink.

She was quirky. She was obsessed with eggs and wanted them for every meal. She would pack food into the side of her cheeks and hold it there for hours. We had to make her spit it out for fear that she would choke. We would also find food hidden in her room, in her tiny purse, and in her shoes. She was determined that she would not ever be hungry. She also tantrumed. Oh my, did she tantrum. Because she had been so sick in China, she was not disciplined and was allowed to do what she wanted to do. No one likes to discipline a child who is ill. Mom and dad telling her **no** was a new thing for MengYan, and something she wasn't fond of!

MengYan did get to be that adorable little flower girl. Brogan and Zachary's wedding was amazing, and Rory as the ring bearer and MengYan as the flower girl made my heart so happy. The wedding was perfect, and, just like that, my oldest child was married!

One beautiful moment actually happened after the wedding. My grandmother, whom we called Mary the Great, was failing in health and was exhausted from the wedding. MengYan was also still weak and was tired out from all the activities. A photographer happened to catch the two of them sitting on a pew, Mary the Great sound asleep with little MengYan asleep on her lap. It is such a beautiful, perfect photo of two people who are so incredibly special to me.

Meng has continued to grow and thrive. As a teenager, she is beautiful and so smart, and has more compassion than any child I have ever seen. She still receives blood transfusions every three weeks at the St. Jude Midwest Affiliate. The staff there have become family to us. Dr. Saving, Dr. Ross, Deedee, and the others… they love her as much as we do.

Meng has never let anything stop her. She runs and wins 5Ks, plays seriously competitive basketball, bikes, and spends a lot of time on the trampoline. She has had struggles. She has had to have her appendix and gallbladder removed. She is on her second medi-port for easy vein access. She has a lot of facial "bossing" from her disease, which has wreaked havoc with her teeth, so braces are in her near future. Despite all of these things, she has joy and reflects that joy to everyone.

MengYan is a blessing from God! She is blessed with an ability to understand and deeply love children, especially children with special needs, and they love her right back. She is my right hand, and God knew I needed her for the children that were coming in our future!

To MengYan, my Chinese princess:
I have never met you,
But I love you.
I have never held or kissed you,
But I cannot wait to.
You do not know me,
But God made you my daughter.
You don't even know it,
But God is preparing your heart for me.
The hand of God is so strong upon you;
He holds you for me.
Let Him comfort you, my sweetheart,
Until I can myself.
Don't be sad, don't feel alone,
We will be there soon!
*His plan for you is **so** great.*
I am blessed and highly favored;
I cannot wait to meet you!
Please, Lord, move mountains and move
time!

Chapter 14

Finding My Daley Faith

There was a family we had come to know through our homeschooling cooperative that had five children. The oldest child, Gabby, was severely disabled, having suffered a devastating birth injury. Although she was now twelve, she could not walk, talk, sit up, or eat by mouth. Dale and I became close to this family, and often they came to our home to visit. Gabby's momma, Jodi, and I would frequently homeschool our kids together.

It was a lot of fun having someone like-minded with which to share ideas and dreams. Jodi's children enjoyed helping with barn chores, and all of our children got along well. But it was Gabby who won my heart. I watched Jodi lovingly care for her daughter. Gabby wore diapers like an infant and needed to be changed often. She ate her meals through a feeding pump that went directly into her stomach. She had seizures, which I learned were not so scary. Many people would look at Gabby and think she was a vegetable, that she had no thoughts or emotions, but the more I spent time with her, the more I realized this was not true. Gabby smiled. She recognized people, especially her mother. She had such a beautiful, sweet spirit, and when I was around her, I felt so close to God. Eventually, I helped Jodi with some of Gabby's care, and I think she began to like me too.

One afternoon, the phone rang. I picked up. "Hello, McKinney residence."
"Is this Mrs. McKinney?"
"Yes, it is."
"Hi, I'm Rebecca,* a caseworker from "CHASK."
Instantly, my ears perked up.

"I am looking for a family for a four-month-old baby girl. She was adopted by a lovely family at birth, but they have just learned that she has lots of medical needs. It's been such a difficult decision, but they have decided to look for a new family for her."

"Okay. Can you tell me more?"

She gave me the details. "When she was about six weeks old, her head began to swell, and she became very fussy and agitated. Her new family took her to the doctor, who then referred her to the Emergency Department. After some tests, and more

124

importantly, an MRI, they found that this baby girl has significant brain deficiencies. Much of her brain is missing, and the remaining space has been filled with cerebrospinal fluid, and that caused her head to swell.

"The baby required emergency surgery to place a shunt in her head, which drains the excess spinal fluid. This prevents further brain damage. The neurologist believes that this child will be severely disabled. She most likely won't ever walk, talk, or be able to care for herself in any way."

I immediately thought of Gabby.

Rebecca continued. "It's been really tough for the parents. They love this little girl, but they are both full-time executives, and this baby will need specialized care twenty-four hours a day. They finally decided to find a new family for this baby."

I listened carefully to everything the caseworker shared with me and could almost feel the weight of the decision those parents had to make. "I can't imagine how difficult that must have been for them, but I must say, I admire their honesty and the fact that they aren't afraid to set boundaries for themselves. Thank you for the call. I want to talk with Dale, and I'll call you back if we think we can parent her."

As I hung up the phone, I was thinking that there was no way we could care for this baby who needed so much care. MengYan had only been home four months, and her health was still frail. She still had volatile temper tantrums almost daily, which was so difficult to handle. I pushed the phone call, and the thought of this baby, to the back of my mind and continued with my day.

I couldn't sleep that night, and I couldn't quit thinking about that baby girl. I felt in my heart that God had put Gabby in my life—even placed her in my home—just to erase my fears and make me comfortable with the idea of parenting a severely disabled child. I prayed a lot. But I wasn't ready to talk to Dale quite yet.

I woke up thinking about that baby and talked with Jodi at length about parenting a disabled child. I wanted to learn as much as I could about what it required. I wasn't sure we were the right family; we were so busy, always on the go. Jodi rarely took Gabby out because it was difficult. That evening I did talk to Dale, and even though we were terrified, we prayed for God to open or close doors.

The more we talked, the more we felt the doors closing. We had no money—MengYan's adoption had taken its toll on our finances, and we were still in budget recovery. Also, we lived in Illinois, a state that had incredibly challenging adoption policies. Illinois policy limited the number of children a family can adopt (at this point, we had seven) and they also were very restrictive about allowing an Illinois family to adopt an out-of-state child that had significant physical or emotional challenges. They were fearful that the child would become a burden to the state. Armed with this information, I made a return call to the caseworker.

"Hi, Rebecca, this is Ann McKinney."
"Hello, Ann. It's good to hear from you. I hope you have a 'Yes!' for me."

"Unfortunately, I just don't see how it would be possible for us to adopt this baby. We simply don't have the money to pay for an adoption."

"Well, Ann, you will be happy to hear that all the fees for this adoption have been waived."

I was surprised, but instantly I thought of the Illinois law and knew that the answer was

127

still no. "That's great, but Illinois will most likely not approve us for this child, since our family size is large, and she is disabled."

"This baby girl **is** in Illinois, so you won't need their approval."
Bam! All of my excuses were gone!

"Wow, I don't know what to say! But I do know that we will continue to pray and talk it through. This is a really big decision. Give me a few days to give you an answer."

Sunday came, and off we went to church. Our pastor's message could not have been for anyone else in that entire church—it was only for us. Pastor Tim preached on not just hearing God's voice but also obeying it. He talked about stepping out in faith even when you are scared, even when it's unfamiliar territory. Dale and I went to the altar after the service to pray and seek God's will. And we decided to accept this baby girl into our family!

Early Monday morning, I called Journeys of Hope, the agency facilitating the adoption of this baby girl. The woman I spoke to was curt and told me that many families had stepped forward to offer this child a home. She would add us to her list, but she was sure there would be no problem placing this child. Wow. I laughed and I cried. What on earth was God doing here? Maybe God wanted to see if we were willing to do this difficult task but didn't want us to actually carry it out. Was He testing us as He tested Abraham, who obeyed God and was prepared to sacrifice his son, Isaac? What a journey we were on. Dale and I were not sure what to do with this crazy twist of events, but we just continued to trust God to lead our family.

On Tuesday morning, Jodi and her family stopped by for a visit. It was great to see them all, especially sweet Gabby, who smiled when I stroked her cheek. I wondered what it would be like to parent a child similar to Gabby. In a way, I was disappointed that this baby girl was not coming to my home. But at least I would still have Gabby to love on.

Just a few hours later, as Dale and the family and I were heading to Champaign for a visit with Rory's birth mother and twin brother, the phone rang. It was the facilitator from Journeys of Hope. She told me that every single family on her list had backed out, and she wanted to know if they could bring the baby to us the following day. At this point, my emotions got the best of me, and I cried and laughed at the same time. I think Dale and the kids were all in shock. I kicked into high gear, my mind racing as I began making lists of things I needed to get quickly. Once we were home, I frantically began cleaning my house to prepare for the social worker and baby who were arriving so soon.

Dale is my rock, and he helped me slow down enough to think and prepare my heart as well as my home. We were all excited at the idea of parenting this baby girl, but we were also terrified. We had received a copy of her medical records and had also spoken to her adoptive momma. So many unknowns surrounded this baby. One report said they did not expect her to live long. Another said that her life expectancy was approximately twelve months. All reports stated that she was expected to be severely disabled. It was estimated that she was missing 60–70 percent of her brain. Her adoptive family had named her Sydney Reese, and she had a fair complexion and blue eyes. Her current momma told us that she was very fussy, very stiff, and hard to feed.

Could I do this? Could **we** do this? This would take a new step of faith every day. A daily faith. And at the moment, while sitting at the dining room table, we realized that God had just given us this baby's name. Her name was to be Daley Faith! We simply changed the spelling of *daily* to compliment her daddy.

Daley Faith arrived at our home the following afternoon. To my surprise, it was not the caseworker who brought her, it was the adoptive family. They carried our baby girl in and brought all of her clothing and toys with them. This little princess was spoiled! I could tell right away that the family loved her so very much, and letting her go was probably one of the hardest decisions they could ever make. I cried as they cried. It touched my heart to know that she had been surrounded by love from day one.

Daley was adorable, but so pale. Actually, she was not really pale, but my last five children were either bi-racial, African American, or Chinese, so this little gal looked pale to me. She was fussy and irritated when I tried to hold her, but Bronwyn and MengYan snatched her away from me, and she calmed down. When we took off her little knit hat, we were surprised at the size of her shunt. I did not expect it to be so prominent. At first, the kids were all afraid to touch it but got used to it quickly.

Daley certainly was a fussy gal. She cried. A lot. She didn't sleep much, either. Homeschooling was a challenge, with this baby girl screaming and fussing so much. I rewrote our homeschool schedule so that we would rotate every thirty minutes, taking turns snuggling and holding her. It was the only way we could get anything accomplished. It took all of us. MengYan was completely in her element. She adored Daley and could diaper her, change her clothes, and feed her like a pro. She was the only child who didn't seem to mind Daley's scream. As I was thinking about this one afternoon, I realized that since Daley had been with us, MengYan had not had another tantrum. We were so busy with Daley that I hadn't noticed.

Watching MengYan with Daley made me understand things more clearly. God revealed to me that MengYan had grown up in an orphanage. She had been doing things for herself for quite some time, even though she was so young. Here I was mothering her so heavily, doing everything for her because she was sick. Instead of making her feel loved and comforted, however, this was upsetting Meng. She had been a caretaker in her orphanage and was not comfortable with things the other way around. Daley had given her back her purpose and had made me shift my smother-mothering off of Meng and onto Daley. MengYan and Daley became quite close very quickly. It was a beautiful thing to watch!

In another strange twist, shortly after Daley became our daughter, Jodi and her family found themselves in-between homes. Dale and I share the gift of hospitality. We like to welcome people and make them feel at home. We like to share what we have, and we cannot stand to see someone in need. This explains why we always have extra people in our home. Throughout the years, we have housed eight Japanese exchange students, several homeless people, and we always have a lot of neighborhood children at our home.

It didn't take much thought or prayer before we offered Jodi and her family a place to stay while they worked through their housing situation. Sweet Gabby, who won my heart and made me feel at ease with her disability, was now living with us. Again, God used Jodi and Gabby to help me feel more at ease as I began to navigate the world of parenting a medically fragile child with severe disabilities.

Doctor appointments with Daley were difficult. I frequently left their offices in tears. Some doctors think that if you did not give birth to the baby, you won't have the same attachment as a birth mother. So often they say things they normally wouldn't and perhaps shouldn't. I recall one particular neurologist. He came into the room with several interns and began to discuss Daley's brain deficiencies with them. He looked me right in the eye and asked if we were seriously adopting Daley, and when I told him yes, he asked if I had seen her MRI. I told him I had. He chuckled and then asked me if I needed an MRI. It blew me away. I could not believe this doctor just said that to me. I did not know what to do, so I got up, put Daley into her car seat, and walked out of the room. I walked right past the receptionist as she asked me if I needed to make another appointment, and I fought to hold back the tears until I got into the car. There were several other doctor appointments like this.

It was not just at doctor appointments where I was left dumbfounded over someone's words. Many of my friends and family members expressed concerns to Dale and me that we had gone too far. They felt that this child would take away from our time and resources for our other children. They thought it would be terrible to have our children watch a sibling die if Daley's life expectancy predictions were accurate. Often, when Daley had cried for hours on end, I would want to ask someone to pray for me or just give me a break for a few hours. Once I did ask a friend, and she somewhat jokingly told me that I had "signed up for this." I never asked again.

It was difficult for us to go anywhere because Daley cried so much. My church gave us a baby shower for Daley, and she cried the entire time. The kids could always find me at Walmart; they would just listen for the screaming baby, and there I was. It was very, very hard. I questioned God many nights over our decision to bring Daley into our family. But when I could get her to settle down, she would look into my eyes, and I felt such peace. And every once in a while, we would see some personality. She would give us a smirky smile or would coo or babble.

Daley's battles were just ugly. She had hydrocephalus, severe brain deficiencies, spastic quad paraplegia, epilepsy, cortical vision impairment, reflux, neurogenic bowel and bladder, and neurological irritability. Most doctors said if she lived to be three, she would most likely calm down and her mood would stabilize. We just had to wait it out.

Daley grew but didn't calm down. She began early intervention therapy services, and we were blessed to have many of the same therapists for her that we had for Rory. Daley rarely interacted during her therapies and really did not make gains. She reached her first birthday and we all celebrated that she had proven her doctors wrong.

It was at about this time that we realized that Becky, the daughter of a friend, had a special touch with Daley. When I could not get Daley to quit crying, usually MengYan could, but we saw over and over that Becky could do the same. So, Becky would frequently come over and just sit and snuggle with Daley to give me a break.

It was at about this time that I took Daley for her one-year checkup. My beloved family doctor could see the exhaustion in my eyes and probably noticed that this child had aged me. He asked me how much she was sleeping and was horrified when I told him one to three hours per night. He reminded me that this was very unhealthy for both of us. He recommended that we put Daley on a mild sedative. At this point, I was willing to try anything. Letting Daley just "cry it out" would not work for her, as it made her more irritated and would often cause her to have a seizure. So, Dr. Wall ordered Daley a medication for sleeping. It was wonderful! With this new medication, Daley would sleep three to four hours at a time, something she had never done. That medication gave me back my life.

When Daley was two, she went into status epilepticus, which is a big, ugly seizure

136

that won't stop. We had been told that this would probably be how she would die, so it was terrifying. After waiting thirty minutes for it to stop and trying all of our emergency medications, we rushed her to our local hospital. An hour later, they still were unable to stop the seizure. She was taken by ambulance to a children's hospital in Peoria, where they put her into a medically induced coma. This finally stopped the seizure. At this point, she had been seizing for almost four hours. Her brain suffered additional damage, and when she awoke from her coma, she had lost most of the ability to swallow. She was also totally blind instead of just visually impaired. Oh, our poor baby girl! But she had shown us that she was much tougher than we knew.

After struggling to get her to swallow even a few milliliters of formula, we had no option but to have a feeding tube surgically placed. She had always been difficult to feed with a bottle, but now it was impossible. Our sweet girl now ate her meals through a tube in her belly, just like Gabby did. It was weird, it was awkward, but it was our life now. All the kids learned to feed her, and soon it became second nature. This feeding tube, although I hated it, saved our girl's life. She would have died without it.

137

Daley continued to grow and to pass all of the life expectancies doctors had placed on her. She continued to have struggles. Her cerebral palsy and tightness caused scoliosis and also caused both of her hips to dislocate. At one point, she had seventy-five or more seizures per day. Her immune system was poor, and sickness hit her much harder than it did our other children. But she was alive! She smiled and sometimes giggled. She loved her siblings, especially her sisters. She had likes and dislikes and favorite toys. She adored her daddy.

And then, when Daley reached the age of four, her crying and her fussiness stopped. Just completely stopped. She became calm, mellow, and more importantly, she became happy! She became a beautiful blessing to our family, and the kids no longer dreaded their thirty minutes with her; they began to fight for the opportunity. We thanked God for seeing us through the Daley storm and slowly adjusted to our new normal. And, little by little, those first stormy years have begun to fade from my memory. I choose to remember the joy she brought me every time she smiled at me or tried to bite me (which was very often, but all in play).

Another blessing was nursing care. Because of the severity of Daley's condition, we found out that she qualified to have a nurse come to our home and help me care for her. At first, this felt weird to me, but we decided to try it. Our first nurse was Tracey. She was wonderful. She helped care for Daley, following all of my instructions, while I homeschooled the other children. It was really a wonderful thing, and such a blessing! Tracey didn't stay too long, though; she was young and had her life ahead of her. She took a traveling nursing job, and we lost her.

Our nursing agency began to look for another nurse for us, but there was quite a shortage. I posted on Facebook that we needed a nurse for a few hours a day, and a homeschool friend let me know that she had someone interested. A few weeks later, we interviewed Miss Sandy.

Miss Sandy had retired from nursing but was just looking for something part-time. I know we overwhelmed her when she first came to our home. My house is a little bit of chaos. There are kids, dogs, and other pets all over my house. Our farm was filled with every farm creature imaginable: horses, cows, goats, sheep, chickens, turkeys, cats, rabbits, and who knows what else!

Daley also overwhelmed Sandy at that first meeting. She was having a "cry-day" and would only stop crying when we would hold her pacifier in her mouth. She could not keep it in on her own, as she had such poor muscle tone. Daley was swinging in her baby swing, and all of us took turns holding in her pacifier and trying to comfort her. We were all used to this way of life, but Sandy was not!

Remarkably, Sandy accepted the job and became Daley's nurse. God knew exactly what He was doing when He sent Sandy to us. She was and still is a huge blessing to my family, and Daley adores her. The day I knew Sandy was perfect for us was the day I heard her praying over Daley as our girl had a hard seizure. It brought tears to my eyes. This skill was worth far more than any nursing skill Sandy had, and she became Daley's personal prayer warrior and nurse.

Daley has far surpassed any life expectancy ever given to her. She is happy and content, and she rarely cries. She has certainly struggled, having had fifteen surgeries in her short life, most of them with complications. But we now have a wonderful team of doctors that work with us and are positive and hopeful rather than counting down the days Daley has left. Just like with Gabby, I feel closer to God when I am close to Daley

Faith. It almost seems as if she radiates God! I do believe they have deep conversations. Sandy, Becky, and Daley's first family—as well as my extended family—have remained a constant support for us as we parent Daley. Without them, this job would be much more difficult.

A lot of people look at Daley and think that she is most certainly our hardest child. Actually, she is the easiest! She doesn't want anything from us but love and affection. She doesn't want an allowance, car keys, or a cell phone. She doesn't get mad at me or hold a grudge. She doesn't care what clothing I put on her or how I style her hair. She just wants to be loved, and that she is. She is my princess, my angel!

Lord, help me to have Your love for children.
Help me see them through Your eyes, not mine.
Break my heart for what breaks yours.
Let me know Your heart!

Chapter 15

The FIVE B's

Daley Faith was such a challenge that we needed to take a break from adopting any more children, although we hoped we could do so at some point. We were sure that having any more newborns was out of the question, as Miss Daley was forever our newborn. We spent several years adjusting and growing, waiting to see what God had in store for us.

Just before Daley's fourth birthday, Kirsten called us regarding a very unique and challenging situation. She was seeking a family for a sibling group of five. **Five!** These kiddos were from the projects of East St Louis and had led a difficult life. They had quite a history of abuse and neglect. They were Brandon, fifteen; Brittany, thirteen; Brianna, twelve Brian, ten; and Bria, three. They became known as the Five B's.

The thought of adding five children to our family of ten was overwhelming, but we agreed to pray as we had in the past: "God please open the doors or close them, as You see fit." But it was intimidating. Five! I wasn't sure we could afford to feed five more kids.

The caseworker Kirsten had assigned to the kids called us about a week later. She was coming to our city for another situation and wanted to know if she could bring Brittany and Brianna to meet us. After a few conversations, the proposed meeting turned into a weekend visit.

Brittany and Brianna were terrified to meet us. Brianna looked like she was going to cry. I remember thinking, *Do I look that scary?* They hopped into our van, and off we went to the farm. Once we got home, they settled in, and then they got excited. They had never been to a farm before. They wanted to see the animals, climb the haystacks, and run through the woods at the park next door.

Brianna and Bronwyn clicked right away, and by the end of the weekend, they were chatting like long-lost sisters. Brittany preferred to talk with Dale and me. She had a lot of questions, one of her first being, why on earth would we have a photo of that horrible man hanging in our living room? We couldn't figure it out until she took us into the living room and pointed at our beloved portrait of George W Bush praying with the twin towers behind him. We are a conservative Christian family, but we quickly learned that these kiddos had not been brought up that way. They hated Republicans, any authority, and the police. Hmmm, this could be difficult!

Overall, we had a good visit. After talking it over with the family, we decided to have all five kids over for the extended Thanksgiving break. As that holiday approached, we stocked up our pantry and frig and then headed off to pick them up.

We had never met Brandon, Brian, or Bria before. Brandon did not appear nervous at all to meet us. He had his bag packed and ready. Brian was terrified. We realized that he was developmentally delayed within a few minutes of meeting him but were unsure as to what extent. Kirsten had not mentioned this to us. Brian was afraid, even when I simply tried to touch his head or stroke his face. Bria was a sweet little sass, the spoiled baby of the family. Her siblings adored her, and she got what she wanted. Her entire diet consisted of chips, soda, and candy because that is what she wanted.

Thanksgiving week was mostly good. Bria was the biggest challenge. She wanted me to rub her back but didn't want to see me because she was afraid of me. I rubbed her back while she hid her face under a pillow. She had a SpongeBob toy that seemed to serve as her "security blanket," and she carried it with her everywhere. And true to form, no matter what I did, I couldn't get her to eat anything even remotely healthy.

Brian mostly played alone, making odd little noises and talking to himself in a strange voice. He ate so much food I could not believe it. He also looked to his brother, Brandon, before making any decision. We did have one incident with Brian when he grabbed Toby and head-butted him. At this point, we took it as roughhousing and dismissed it.

Brandon kept it cool all weekend and tried his best to impress us with his street stories. The girls got along very well, making music videos and movies on their iPods.

We took the kids to church that Sunday in hopes that someone there might decide they needed to adopt a sibling group of five. That did not happen. Even our pastor's wife, who sincerely wanted to adopt, could not wrap her head around **five** at once! We did get a surprise after church, however. Someone had stocked our van full of food. Good food! Name brand food, which this momma did not normally buy. The kids were thrilled; what a blessing!

The days flew by, and the time came to return them to their home in East St. Louis. We said our goodbyes and waited to see what would happen next. We did not feel called to parent all five, for various reasons, but we were open and willing to whatever God chose for our family. Again, we prayed, "God, open or close these doors, and bless these children!"

The following week, Kirsten called us with the news that the children's mother had decided not to place them with a family. She was working on a way to continue to parent them. We considered the door closed, but we wanted to help support her in any way we could. We put the message out at church that we wanted to provide Christmas for the Five B's and their mother and grandmother. We were overwhelmed with beautiful, amazing, and generous gifts. Our church family really came through!

A few days before Christmas, we made arrangements to meet the mother and kids at the adoption agency, and we literally filled their van. It was so much fun! And it was so good for our kids to experience the blessing of helping others.

Just before Valentine's Day, the Five B's mother called me.

"Hello, Ann? This is Denice.* I've changed my mind, and I want you and Dale to adopt the kids."

My mind raced as I tried to absorb what she was saying. "Um... well, are you sure about this, Denice? How about you take a little more time and think about it?"

Her answer was without hesitation. "No, I've made up my mind."

I tried again. "Denise, what can Dale and I do to help you parent the kids? Do you need help with groceries? Rent? Utility bills? We really do want to help you."

"No, Ann, I just cannot do this anymore. I need you to come and get them. Please. I can have them ready this evening. And I will sign whatever paperwork needs to be signed. I need them to have a better life than I can give them. Please just say yes.

My heart broke over the desperation I could hear in her voice.

A few days later, we officially accepted guardianship of the Five B's with the intent to adopt them all. And people thought we were crazy before… I can only imagine the thoughts of people who didn't understand obedience to the Lord.

The first thing we worked on was living arrangements. We shuffled bedrooms around, made arrangements to pick up donated bunk beds, and made sure we had enough bedding to go around.

Next came school. This was so much harder. Brandon, Brittany, and Brianna had missed almost three years of school. They all loved to read and their reading and comprehension were fantastic, but their mathematics and grammar skills were far behind. I put all three through educational assessments to determine where to begin with their homeschool education. I knew Brian needed to be in school but homeschooling him was not possible. He did not speak well, had his own language for many things, and could not read even short vowel words at the age of ten. And Bria just needed to play and be a toddler for a bit. She was not ready for anything formal.

A few days after our church family got word that the Five B's were with us, my friend Heather called. Heather and her husband had two biological children and had adopted a son through foster care. Their adopted son was African American, and they did not want him to be the only coffee-colored member of the family. They asked if we would consider letting them adopt Bria.

As soon as the words came from Heather's lips, I felt complete and total peace. This family was perfect for Bria! She would be the baby of the family and would be adored by her older siblings. They were financially stable, and Heather was a counselor, so she would be a tremendous asset to Bria as she matured and had questions about her early years.

The Townsend family picked up Bria the following day and began transitioning her into their family as their new daughter. We agreed to always make sure the siblings had as much contact as they wanted and needed. Brittany was torn over letting Bria go, but she also felt that this was God-ordained and a very good situation for Bria.

The following week, a woman from church began asking a lot of questions about

Brandon and about adoption. She and her husband had older children, all older than Brandon, and they had no children together, as they were both widowed and recently married. They asked if Brandon could come to their Super Bowl party so they could become better acquainted with him.

Brandon began spending more and more time with this family, and it finally got to the point where they asked if they could adopt him. Again, the peace of God came over Dale and me, and we knew in our hearts that this was right. Brandon moved in with Marsha and Kent's family, and for the first time in his life, he became the "little" brother.

And then there were three. Brittany and Brianna settled into a homeschool program and began transitioning into our family. Brian was enrolled in a life skills program through the public-school system and began adjusting to his new life.

Throughout this process, God touched and blessed us through others. Very often, we came out to our van to find it full of groceries. I would find envelopes of money in our mailbox. On the rare occasions when we ate dinner at a restaurant, it was not unusual for some random stranger to pay our bill. This was God's blessing.

Since this adoption was a private one, there was no assistance with paying the legal fees, and they were substantial. We completed many fundraisers over the course of time it took to officially adopt the B's. And in the end, God stretched our budget, blessed us through generous family and friends, and covered all of our needs. God is good. God wants His children in families.

Dear sweet Lord, my children can't sleep,
Please send an angel to rest at their feet.
Send another angel to stroke their hair,
Help them feel your presence there.
Calm their minds of all their fears,
Hold them when they come to tears.
Help them feel so safe and sound,
Let them feel your love surround.
In Your hands, my children will be
You love them, Lord, even more than me

*Name has been changed

Chapter 16

Brittany Rae

Brittany, the oldest girl of the Five B's, was thirteen when she came to us. She was a smart girl and very mature for her age. She was naturally beautiful, and people would frequently tell her she should pursue a modeling career.

Shortly after getting to know Brittany, Dale and I realized that she was the glue that held this sibling group together. She cared for all of her younger siblings just like a mother would. She told me stories of winters when they had no heat, days without food, and many times when there was no adult in their home for extended amounts of time. But Brittany had kept things together because she loved her family. She was a rock!

One evening, Dale and I were in the kitchen when Brittany came in, a hesitant look on her face. "Um… can I tell you something?"

"Sure, Brittany," Dale replied. As we sat down at the counter, I could tell something was bothering her.

"Well," she said, "something happened a while ago when we were still at home, and I just need to tell you about it.

"Mom had been gone for almost a week, and we didn't know where she was or when she was coming back. We were all really hungry, and there wasn't anything left in the house to eat. I just kept thinking, *ALDI'S is so close; I just wish I could go there and get something,* but we didn't have any money."

Brittany hesitated, and tears rolled down her cheeks. "Finally, I put on one of mom's wigs, took one of her old purses that was lying around, and walked to ALDIS. I took Brian and Bria with me. I knew I had to keep them safe, so I made them hold my hands.

"You know how you have to have a quarter to get a cart? Well, when we got there, I stood by the cart rack and waited until a lady was walking in, then I dug around in the purse a little and said, 'Oh no, I don't have a quarter!' Well, the lady gave me a quarter, so I waited until she was inside, then I did the same thing again. I did that over and over until people had given me enough quarters to buy some hot dogs and chips."

Brittany buried her face in her hands and sobbed. "I know it was wrong, and it's so embarrassing, but I just didn't know what else to do!"

My heart ached as I hugged her. "Oh, Brittany, you don't have to feel bad! At least you didn't steal anything, and that's good, right?" I cupped her chin in my hand and raised her face to look at me. "We're so proud of you for taking care of your family! There's many people that wouldn't have been so resourceful, and you did the very best you could."

Brittany was immensely talented. Her drawings were amazing, and she quickly learned to play the guitar and piano. She was so very affectionate and loving with all of the kids, especially Daley Faith and Rory.

But there was a troubled side to Brittany. Of all the kids, she struggled the most with being abandoned by her mother. She missed her dearly, despite how awful the situation was in her home.

Brittany rebelled against authority. She endured horrible nightmares. She had a very low self-image and could not see how beautiful she was. She thought she was overweight. She hated her nose, her legs, her height. No matter what we did, we could not convince her that she was perfect. We hired numerous counselors for her, but she was never receptive to talking to them, so no progress was made. Her obsession with her weight turned into an eating disorder, for which we became very concerned.

After some time, Brittany confessed something we had suspected all along: she had been sexually abused for most of her life. Her abuser was a family member to whom she was very close. It had broken her spirit and caused horrible depression and hate in her heart. We were so thankful that she trusted us enough to confide in us, but we were overwhelmed, as this was a totally new area for us. We reached out to counselors, therapists, and teachers, grasping for ways to help our Brittany.

Brittany's mental state did not improve. It became more and more of a struggle for her. Once the kids became old enough for high school, we placed them in a wonderful Christian school in our community, but even this was a challenge for her. Some days she could not get through a day of school without grief and ideas of self-harm overcoming her.

Dale and I prayed. We tried everything that came to our minds to help her. We begged God for guidance, but she seemed to pull away from us more and more as she got older. I know that Dale and I made a lot of mistakes with Brittany; we felt so totally out of our element. We could handle physical challenges with our children with no hesitation, but this was so much harder. Fighting invisible demons is the hardest thing I have ever done. It was and is utterly heartbreaking.

More and more, Brittany began to see Dale and me as the enemy. Oh, Lord, we wanted nothing more than the best for her, but she just couldn't see that. We tried the things we thought would help her: dance classes, guitar lessons, vocal lessons, cheerleading, volleyball, and art classes. She lost interest in all of them and began a spiral into the dark. She refused to take medications that our family doctor prescribed for her, which made things even worse. She was convinced that all of these things were an attempt to completely control her. She did not see them for what they were, desperate attempts to show her our love.

When Brittany turned nineteen, she felt she could not be around us anymore and moved in with a family friend. Things there were rocky as well, and she bounced around to several different friends' homes over the next few months.

We loved and missed her dearly and, at one point, talked with her about moving back home. She, however, had no interest in conforming to our house rules. She wanted to do what she wanted whenever she wanted.

Our hearts broke as we lost touch with Brittany. She found a man to help her relocate to Missouri and, eventually, Memphis. We do hear from her occasionally. When we do, she tethers back and forth between missing us and being angry at us.

Despite everything, we have absolutely no regrets. Brittany is a treasure. She is our daughter forever, and we love her so much. This is not at all the way we thought our lives with her would look. The more we pray for Brittany, the more we know she is our Prodigal, and God's hand is upon her. He has protected her from so much in her life and helped her be strong and brave, and we know that this separation is not forever. We trust Brittany into God's hands, and we trust Him to bring her back to us when she is ready. We miss you so much, Brittany! Come home!

Brittany:
The Lord delights in you,
He sings for you.
He knew you in the womb,
He has your hairs numbered.
He knows your future,
He gives strength to you.
He lifts the weary,
He heals the sick.
He died for you,
He blesses you.
He was born for you,
He gave himself for you.
He hears our prayers,
He sends his angels to protect you.
He will not leave or forsake you,
He knows you—yet he loves you.
He will never change,
He forgives and forgets.
He grants peace,
He does great wonders.
He will vindicate you,
He will deliver you from distress.
His love is unfailing,
He is faithful and just.
He is always at work,
He loves you!

Chapter 17

Bri

Brianna is the middle girl of the Five B's. She became part of our family when she was twelve. Brianna was the quiet one, the more fearful one, but also the silly one! She and Bronwyn became close very quickly, and we never knew what those girls were up to. They were forever having lemonade stands, trying to hatch baby chicks, or pretending to be cowboys. They made crazy music videos, which I use to embarrass them to this day.

Through the many stories the Five B's told us, it was evident that their grandmother, known as Nanny, physically abused Brianna. For some reason, Nanny did not care for Brianna. She was beaten often, sometimes severely, and usually over insignificant things. I shudder even to write this, but Brittany claims it was because Brianna had the darkest skin. This horrifies me. Brittany also told us that the same trusted family member also sexually abused Brianna. But Brianna did not dwell on her sorrow and painful past the way

Brittany did. Brianna was always happy, always smiling, always up to something!

When we first attempted to talk to Brianna about the alleged abuse, she denied it all, especially the sexual abuse. But as time went by and she learned to trust us more, she began to talk about the physical abuse. She told us of the beatings and the times she was forced to go without food or denied use of the bathroom. At times, Nanny even encouraged the other children to attack and hurt Brianna. The crazy thing is that Brianna didn't seem to harbor hate or anger in her heart, although she has no desire to ever see her mother or Nanny again.

I thanked God for giving her such a forgiving spirit, but I also feared that the hate and anger might rear its ugly head in her future. We enrolled Brianna in counseling, and she did very well. But she didn't open up about any sexual abuse, which made us wonder if it really happened.

Then one day, as I was cooking dinner, Brianna came into the kitchen. The room was full of kids, as always, and it was noisy and a bit chaotic. Brianna walked over to me and began to talk about the sexual abuse. It was so strange to me that she would choose this busy moment to tell me the things from her heart, but looking back, I see this was safe for her. She knew I was not in a position to ask more questions or to pump her for details. It was her way of controlling the conversation. She was a smart girl. What she did say was the most mature thing I think she has ever said to me. She said, "What happened to me was in the past, and I am living for my future." She had wisdom beyond her years.

Brianna has a very unique charisma, with a beautiful smile, a spunky spirit, and a motivation to find her path in this world. Proving herself a good student, she was the star of her volleyball team and Prom Queen in her senior year of high school. She has more friends than I have ever dreamed of having, loves her siblings, and is a loyal daughter. Graduating from a Dental Assisting program, she began her career in the dental industry.

I thank God for holding her tight during her dark, formative years and for speaking forgiveness into her spirit. I thank Him for giving her joy, and I pray that as she grows, she will continue to live for her future and let go of her past. Brianna is a beautiful gift to me!

Homeschooling, Bible verses, learning to count,
These are the things that my life is about.
Diapers, laundry, and trips to the mall,
Being a mom means doing it all.
Ice cream, real tears, and expensive new glasses,
To learn all these things,
There are no special classes.
Ringing phones, bike rides, and sweet chubby tummies,
Even cleaning those old, nasty bathroom scummies.
I'm tired, I'm sore and I need a vacation,
But I must say, I simply love my mom occupation.

Chapter 18

Brian Lamont

Brian came to us at the age of ten, and we loved him right away. He was sweet, quirky, and affectionate. He seemed to crave physical touch once he realized it was not painful. He was always smiling and tried his best to do what the other boys did.

However, from day one in our home, he was a mystery to me. It took many doctors and many evaluations, but at the onset of school, he was diagnosed with autism, moderate mental impairment, post-traumatic stress disorder, and anxiety. As he grew older, more diagnoses would be added to that list.

Brian's school records, which were few, were troubling. He was defiant, aggressive, and could not or would not learn. His birth mother had ignored attempts to get him additional help from the school district. There was also a journal that his kindergarten teacher had kept, documenting his odd behaviors and aggression. This was very disturbing to us, but we walked in faith and prayed that the stability of a family would heal Brian.

163

We enrolled him in a Life Skills classroom at the local public school, and he thrived for the first few years. He learned to read and write and quickly caught up on his math skills. He adored his teacher, Mrs. Morgan, and she did an excellent job of educating our boy. For the first time in his life, school became something he loved.

Brian also adored telling knock-knock jokes, even if they made no sense, and loved reading anything he could about wild animals. He would spend hours on the computer, watching videos of animals in their natural environment.

We knew the PTSD and anxiety were most likely from an abusive childhood, but his autism and mental impairment were puzzling. Nanny had physically abused him, but unlike Brianna, he still held a devotion to her and missed her dearly. Brittany and Brianna told me that many times he was swung into the wall headfirst as a punishment. They also told me that he was very fussy and difficult as an infant, so their mom had them fill his baby bottle with beer and allow him to drink as much as he wanted until he fell asleep. He could have suffered brain damage from either trauma or alcohol.

The sisters also told me that they have an uncle whose condition is very similar to Brian's, so there could have been a hereditary factor as well. Another strike against Brian was his constant exposure to horror movies from a very young age. His family would watch horror movies for fun and then turn off the lights and reenact them. This terrified Brian. He struggled to know what was real and what was pretend.

There were oddities about Brian that I wish I had paid more attention to. He had complete conversations with himself, using different voices; many times, it seemed to be even a different language. He had his own names for things; a tornado was a TeeTock, and a monster truck was a Jamonk. He played best by himself and would often tell me he was attacked by flying dinosaurs on the playground.

One day, as Brian walked in the door after school, I noticed that he had a peculiar, stiff-legged gait.

"What's wrong, Brian? Did you hurt yourself today?"

He looked up at me, eyes wide. "No, Mom, you won't believe what happened! I was just sitting in my seat on the way home when, all of a sudden, there was a rattlesnake on the floor, right between my feet! It was all curled up and was lookin' right at me, and I knew that if I moved, it was finna bite me! So, I just held really, really still all the way home. Now my legs are sore."

I laughed. "Okay, Brian, I'm just glad it didn't bite you!" That boy had such an imagination! *He surely does like his pretend games*, I thought.

Once, we smelled a strong smell of urine coming from Brian's bedroom. We searched his bedding, thinking he had peed his bed the previous evening, but everything was dry. We continued to smell the urine for several days. Finally, Dale and I decided to investigate further. e moved his bed out from the wall and discovered that he had been peeing down his wall, and it had puddled under his bed. This had been going on for some time. When we questioned him about it, he told us that a man waited for him each night in the bathroom and was planning to slit his throat. He had to pee down his wall to stay safe.

Other things were red flags to us as well. We would see young children at the store, and Brian would hide behind me, afraid that they would hurt him. We took Brian to see a psychotherapist. She helped us better understand his disability and prescribed some medications for Brian to help with his anxiety and fears.

When Brian began to go through puberty, things changed. He grew so fast and became very strong, but his attitude became worse. He didn't understand why he couldn't go to the same school as his siblings and didn't like learning at a younger level. He got angry because we no longer left him alone with the younger children and began to have violent outbursts, going from smiling to screaming in a matter of seconds. Usually, I could calm him down by distracting him or redirecting his attention, and his doctor changed and increased his medication.

The first time Brian struck me was during a youth party at our home. We had about fifteen teens over, and it was a great party. Brian began running and chasing the other teens, and I could tell he was getting too rough. I met him at the top of the stairs and asked him to calm down and asked him to help me serve the ice cream. He got inches from my face and began screaming in a deep, terrible, angry voice. I put my hand on his chest and attempted to move him away from me. He grabbed my hand, slapped me, and then pushed me down the steps. Brittany tried to intervene, and he struck her as well. Needless to say, the party was over.

This was just the first of the violence Brian exhibited. He attacked Dale multiple times over the following year and attacked Toby many times, causing him to have sickle cell pain crises. He raged any time he did not like what we were saying or doing or any time he did not get what he wanted. Sometimes he raged for no reason at all. It was horrible.

Brian's violence escalated to the point of being very dangerous. By this point, Brian was almost six-foot tall and weighed 200 pounds. We needed the police department's help on several occasions, and many times he would attack the police officers as well. He was hospitalized for aggression frequently.

Often, when Brian would rage, he would call me Nanny. Always when he raged, his voice was different, and he would say things that were not accurate. He thought people were trying to kill him or were plotting against him. When I gave him his nightly medications, he believed I was trying to poison him. The doctors who provided care for Brian presented the idea of paranoid schizophrenia as a potential diagnosis, and once again, his medications were changed.

The violence continued in our home. It got to the point where we had a "Rage Plan." When Brian began to rage, each big kid took their assigned little kid to the van and locked themselves in. They were not allowed to come out until we gave them the all-clear or the police had Brian in custody.

MengYan and Rory both began having nightmares. I began having anxiety attacks. We were living on eggshells, and we all knew we couldn't do this much longer. Oh, Brian, I always thought you would be my Gentle Giant, my protector and my best pal. I have to admit that I felt very abandoned by God during this time. I have never prayed more for anyone in my life than I did—and still do—for Brian. This was not the way it was supposed to be!

The last night Brian was in our home was a beautiful fall evening. Dale had picked up pizzas for dinner, and we were all ready to eat them. I was sitting down, holding Daley Faith, when Brian began to rage at Dale for some unknown reason. I spoke to Brian, trying to calm him down. He came toward me with fists clenched, and all I could do was cover Daley with both arms. Dale, Brittany, and Patrick were able to stop Brian before he got to Daley and me, but the whole thing escalated quickly, and we had to involve the police again. Dale followed the police and ambulance as they escorted Brian to the hospital. I did my best to regain my composure and get the kids fed and ready for bed.

Dale stayed at the hospital with Brian late into the night, trying to get him the care we knew he needed. I went to bed. As I lay there praying and pleading with God to show me what to do next, I began having chest pains. Incredible chest pains. I could barely breathe, and they continued to get stronger. I thought I was having a heart attack.

As I prayed for God to touch me, I heard Daley begin to cry. All I could think of was that I was dying of a heart attack, begging God to heal me, and instead, Daley needed me now. I pulled myself from my bed, gathered up Daley Faith and her blanket, and carried her to my bed, my chest throbbing with pain the entire time. The minute we laid down Daley began to snuggle herself up to me. This was crazy, because Daley cannot move that well. She was moving in a way I had never seen her maneuver herself.   The minute she snuggled her head into my chest and neck, my pain subsided. It was completely gone. She smiled a precious smile at me, and I knew God had used her to stop my pain. I cried tears of thankfulness, tears of joy, and still some tears of fear, but I felt empowered because I knew God was listening and still in control!

We attempted to get Brian into a treatment facility, but insurance did not cover the cost, and it was not affordable. I don't know who could ever afford this care, as it was 75 percent of Dale's yearly salary. We were pushed into a corner at this point. The state's attorney and police department told us that if Brian injured one of our other children, they could charge us with child endangerment since we knew full well what he was capable of. On the other hand, DCFS said if we didn't continue to parent him in our home, they could charge us with child abandonment. Either way was not good. After tremendous amounts of prayer, we chose not to bring Brian home when he was discharged from the hospital. We loved Brian, but we were fearful he would seriously hurt or kill one of the younger children. And we knew he needed help that we could not afford.

The action we took is called a lock-out. When we chose not to bring Brian home, the police and DCFS were contacted. DCFS took temporary custody of Brian, and Dale and

I were summoned to court the following Monday for child abandonment. The police understood our position and apologized for putting us in this situation. It was a new and sorrowful experience for us. Not having Brian gave us all peace, and we could finally relax in our home. But it was so devastating, as this was not what we thought parenting Brian would ever look like. We were worried about him. Was he okay? Where was he? Did he understand? Did he think we were walking away from him just like his birth mother had done?

Dale and I headed to court on Monday, armed with every single document pertaining to Brian's care, his diagnoses, and a journal of behaviors and rages that Brian had exhibited in our care. The judge who took our case was most gracious. He looked over our documents, saw the fear and weariness in our eyes, and chose not to charge us with abandonment. He knew we had already been through enough and had exhausted our resources. I wondered if he would ever know how much prayer had preceded his decision. He then talked to us about our options. He recommended that we terminate our parental rights and let Brian become a ward of the state. We just couldn't do this! We know God chose us to be Brian's parents, no matter how it might look. Instead, we consulted with an attorney and executed a petition of dependency. This enabled Brian to receive state benefits so he could be placed in a mental health facility for help but also allowed us to retain our voice and our legal rights as his parents. In essence, we became co-guardians with the state of Illinois.

There was a lot of condemnation from people in our circle. Most of them could not understand or chose not to understand. Some felt we were giving up on Brian. Others thought we should have terminated our rights and walked away. In the end, we chose what God put on our hearts and closed our ears to the outside voices. We love Brian, but his behaviors were destroying our family and putting all of us in danger. Brian needed help. We had to get him the help he desperately needed before he seriously hurt someone and faced criminal charges.

Brian bounced around to several facilities. Some were amazing, some were terrible. We found out quickly that resources for kids like Brian are difficult to find, and if you do find them, the waiting list is long. He finally landed at a facility in southern Illinois. He has had both great days and horrible days there. Attempts to place him in a specialized foster home or in a step-down facility were disastrous. But after some time, he finally settled into a program that met his needs.

We are very blessed to be able to continue our relationship with Brian. We visit him once a month, and he can visit us in Decatur once a month. We talk on the phone several times a week. Most of our conversations are pleasant, but occasionally he rages over the phone, especially if he asks for something to which we cannot agree. In those instances, we simply end the call, and normally, by the next call, he has forgotten the previous issue. As a reward for good behavior at his facility, we will frequently pick him up and go for a day trip to St. Louis or similar destinations.

Brian has been one of the most difficult challenges Dale and I have ever endured. But Brian is a child of God. We know beyond a shadow of a doubt that we were put into Brian's life to remove him from a situation of abuse and neglect and get him the help he needed. He has a forever family in us, even if it looks different than any of us anticipated. Brian Lamont is very special, and we pray every day that God will heal his heart from past trauma, restore his clarity of mind, and help him be the man God called him to be. God bless you, Brian!

Ann L. McKinney

I'm sorry that I doubt you, Lord,
I'm sorry that I do.
You've asked me so many times,
To put my trust in you

So many times I try to make it
Better by myself.
While my Bible full of wisdom
Sits on my bedroom shelf

Help me to do better, Lord,
Help me to let go.
To give my stress to you, dear God,
And watch my faith grow.

175

Chapter 19

Landon Nelson

A few months after Brittany, Brianna, and Brian joined our family, Brogan and her husband, Zachary, found out they were pregnant. I was going to be a grandma! Brogan and Zachary were now living in North Carolina, way too far from me.

As the months crept by, Brogan continually sent us updates on her progress and pics of her sweet baby's ultrasounds. This pregnancy was a healing touch from God, as Brogan was still grieving a miscarriage from the previous year. She was handling her pregnancy wonderfully, and we were **so** excited! We brought her back to Illinois to give her a baby shower, which was so much fun for all us girls.

Dale and I sat down with the calendar and planned a Brogan visit. We hoped the timing would work out so we could be there for the baby's birth, or just afterward, so we could help Brogan and Zachary through the first week or two of being new parents. We came up with a date that worked for all of us and found the perfect house to rent. Hotels were out of the question with this brood. We were now a family of thirteen, with eleven of us still living at home. We needed lots of space and a kitchen, so we didn't bankrupt ourselves eating out at every meal.

Soon the time arrived for Brogan to give birth and for us to travel. Brogan had not experienced many early contractions at this point, so we assumed this baby was going to be late, like his momma. We drove our trusty van the thirteen hours to North Carolina and made ourselves comfortable in the rental home. Brogans' birthday was also coming, so even if we were not there for the baby's birth, we could still help Brogan celebrate her birthday.

On the morning of Brogan's birthday, she called from the hospital to let us know that her labor had started, but it was not progressing very quickly. I asked if I could come be with her, but she had decided to head back home and try to speed up her labor instead of sitting in the hospital for hours. I remember laughing as she told me she got a large ball to bounce on to increase contractions. Picturing her bouncing on that ball with her big belly amused me.

By early evening, she went back to the hospital, as her contractions had increased and she progressed into active labor. Zachary told me he would call me when the baby was born. I have to admit, I was disappointed. I was heartbroken, really. I wanted to be there with my baby while she had a baby. But Zachary wanted it to be a private birth, and I respected his wishes. That didn't last long. As the contractions became more painful and more frequent, Brogan wanted her momma, and Zachary called me and asked me to come to the hospital.

Bronwyn, who was twelve at this point, went to the hospital with me. She still thought boys were disgusting and was really grossed out by the idea of childbirth. She kept us all laughing over her queasy stomach and nausea when she thought too hard about it. When delivery time came, we banished Bronwyn to the waiting room, and the main event began. My grandchild was going to be born on his mother's birthday; how special!

Brogan was a champ at childbirth, and even though she was exhausted, she pushed with all her might. It didn't seem like she pushed too long before we saw the sweet little head of my first grandchild. And then he was born: Landon Nelson New.

My first and only grandson had arrived, and he was perfect! Being in the delivery room when Landon made his entrance into this world was one of the most special moments of my life. I thank God for letting me be there, for timing our trip perfectly, and for softening Zachary's heart to my presence.

Landon is amazing. He is so cute, so smart, so big! He has the same compassion as his momma and adores animals and loves them with all his heart. They live in Texas now, so I still don't see him often enough, but he is here most holidays and stays with us for several months each summer.

Being a mom is amazing. Being a grandma is even more amazing! I pray that God will bless me with many more grandchildren, and I pray that He helps me afford to spoil them all.

Landon Nelson, you made my day!
I'm a grandma now, what can I say?
This is a new adventure for me,
But I'm as happy as can be!
I thank God for your health, for your cuteness
too.
You're the most amazing grandson, you know
it's true.
I love when you visit, it brings me such joy.
You're my very favorite little Texan boy!
I hope you know that God loves you,
He made you to be my sweet baboo!

Chapter 20

Wen and Wu: Twins Again!

Not long after the completion of our adoption with Brittany, Brianna, and Brian, our previous international adoption agency sent us an email asking us to consider adopting twins. These twins were both boys, both had arm and hand differences like Rory, and both were totally adorable. We were instantly smitten.

We would have loved to adopt them, but we were knee-deep in the struggles with Brian and still recovering financially from the adoption costs for the three B's. We printed out the boy's photo and placed it on our prayer door. This reminded us to pray for them every day. We prayed that they would find a family. We prayed that they would be loved and well cared for while they waited. Darn, they were so cute!

Our prayer door was a special door in our homeschool room. It was actually my kitchen door. On this door we posted our Bible memory verses, our weekly calendar, and any special prayer requests. These twins, who were known as Logan and Leon, joined another boy from China on our door. The other boy was Teddy, a boy from MengYan's orphanage who was severely disabled. God had put him on my heart when we met MengYan, and we became his sponsor, sending money to help with his care each month. You will learn more about him in the next few chapters.

Time went by, and another agency began advocating for these twins. They changed their names to Ben and Adam. And then another agency picked them up and called them Ping and Pong, which we thought was terrible. Finally, we received word that a family from Holland was pursuing their adoption. We were happy for them, but honestly, my heart was grieved. I felt like they were supposed to be mine. But God had closed that door, and I tried hard to accept it. Our prayers changed, and we began to pray that their family would be perfect for them and that they would grow to be strong and healthy and come to know Jesus.

God must have chuckled over my grieving heart; little did I know that they **were** my twins. He just knew that the timing was wrong. Just after Christmas, the situation with Brian had resolved, and he was safely living in a treatment facility. Our family was working hard to resume normal life. We hadn't even thought about adoption, mainly because we were still in recovery and rebuilding mode.

And then, out of the blue, my good friend Michelle called me. I wasn't surprised to hear from her because she and I were fellow adoption advocates and frequently worked together to find homes for children. She was calling to tell me about some children she hoped we would commit to. She let me know that the twins, Leon and Logan, were once again available for adoption. The family from Holland had backed out after seeing the extent of their differences. Oh, my, here we go again! That door was not closed.

It didn't take much prayer or discussion before the entire family voted an excited **yes** to adopting the twins! We contacted the adoption agency and officially locked their file. We had no idea where we would come up with the $40,000 that we needed to bring them home or where we would put them, as our five-bedroom farmhouse was bursting at the seams. But we stepped out in faith and began the process of bringing these boys home.

When we finally received their official adoption files, we read them front to back dozens of times. The twins were found in a box on the steps of the orphanage as newborn infants. Twin A was Ji Le Wen. He had three fingers per hand and also an undescended testicle. Twin B was Ji Le Wu. He had one finger on one hand, two fingers on the other, and elbows that were locked in place. He also had a strawberry birthmark on his forehead. The photos in their files were absolutely adorable; they looked happy, healthy, and curious. They were almost three years old when we began the adventure of bringing them home.

A surprise complication arose when the caseworker arrived to update our home study. She informed us that our home did not have enough square footage to accommodate two more children legally. We would have to either build an addition onto our house or relocate. We were already trying to figure out how to pay the adoption fees, and now we needed to figure out whether to move or add onto our house. Trusting God, we sought His will.

We got several bids to have an addition built onto our home, and they were much higher than we expected. Dale and I spent a lot of time in prayer over whether we should relocate. I was already feeling the pressure of homeschooling all of the children, caring for

Daley, and maintaining the needs of the farm, and now we were adding twin boys. I felt we had reached the point where we should give up the farm and relocate. But how on earth would we ever find a house big enough to accommodate all of us? And if we could find a house, could we afford it?

We contacted our relator friend, Brenda, and set her to work searching for a house that could accommodate a family of twelve. Brenda presented us with three houses to look at. Number three was it. The minute we walked into it, we knew it was our house. With a few modifications, we could easily make it into a nine-bedroom house! It needed a lot of work, as it had been in bankruptcy many times in the past few years, but it was livable and affordable. We took a giant leap of faith and made an offer on it, which was accepted after just a few counter offers. God moved again, and after showing our farmhouse several dozen times, we received three offers on the farm in one day. And just like that, we became city slickers.

Saying goodbye to my beloved critters—especially my donkey, Pedro—was incredibly hard. My sweet Pedro went to live with my friend Stephanie, who had started Dale and me on this long adoption journey way back with

Keagan! We said tearful goodbyes to our critters and prepared for this new chapter in our lives. We were ready to get those twin boys home.

Our paperwork crept along slowly, as it always does in international adoptions. We received many updates and even a few videos of our boys. They were priceless to us. We had decided to name them Cecil Le Wen (after my father) and Ervin Le Wu (after my father-in-law), but we would call them by their Chinese names, Wen and Wu.

We bought clothes, decorated their rooms, and worked our tails off fundraising to pay the adoption fees. We sold cupcakes, had rummage sales, sold bracelets, had an online auction, and applied for every grant we could find. Little by little, funds began to come in. Even our tax return was much more than expected and was put towards our fees. We feared that, for the first time, we would need to acquire an adoption loan, but God came through. We were in awe of how God moved mountains. We never missed a payment deadline and were never short in paying any of the fees associated with the adoption. In less than ten months, we raised $40,000 through the generosity of God's people and a whole lot of fundraising. This was a miracle!

Finally, in October of 2014, the day came when we got the official invitation to travel to China to bring the boys home. We were so excited to meet our new sons and to visit this beautiful country again. Brogan and Landon flew home to help care for the kids. Dale and I gave everyone tons of hugs and kisses and headed to the airport. Once again, Dale's flight anxiety kicked in, but I kept him well-medicated for that fourteen-hour flight. Everything went perfect as we landed in China, met our guide, and taxied to our hotel. We were meeting our boys the following morning. We were both exhausted, but almost too excited to sleep.

Early the next morning, we were escorted to a room filled with waiting parents. One at a time, children we brought out and introduced to their new families. Some children were excited, and some were terrified. Almost every adult in the room was crying tears of joy. This was a very different situation from when we met MengYan. We found out this was the typical way families met their children. We watched as more and more children met their families.

We finally caught a glimpse of our boys. They were so tiny! They were dressed in identical outfits, but one was red and the other green. They were also wearing girls yellow jelly sandals, which made us both chuckle. As they were brought to us, we could see terror in their eyes. Wen immediately began to cry and reach for his ayi (nanny), and that made Wu begin to cry too. Dale and I tried talking to them, snuggling them, and tickling them, but still they cried. Then I got the crazy idea of putting my glasses on Wu, and they both thought this was hysterical! They laughed and laughed, and they both wanted to wear my glasses. Then they wanted to wear Dale's glasses. They giggled and stopped crying.

The fear returned as Dale and I carried them from the building to the waiting taxi. They were intrigued by the taxi ride and the fancy hotel we were staying in, but the moment we got them to the room, they were, again, very frightened. I could only imagine their fear. They had known us for only a short time, and now they were alone with us. We looked different, smelled different, and talked different. We were scary!

In an attempt to ease their fear, we offered them the arsenal of toys we had brought for them. They wanted to play but were intimidated to take the toys from us. After a bit, Wu dragged Wen behind a lamp, and they had an entire conversation about us. We watched them as they pointed at us and chatted for quite some time. They must have decided we were okay because they came out from behind the lamp, took the toys from us, and began to play.

That evening we took the boys out for dinner, and we could not believe how much they ate. They devoured noodles and congee (rice porridge) but didn't care for French fries. We were impressed with how well Wu could use his spoon and fork, considering he had only three fingers. Wen had no difficulties at all. His differences were very mild.

Our time in China was amazing. The boys were so well behaved and never cried again after that first day. They **loved** to take baths and they loved to eat. Every day, Dale and I would load them into their strollers and explore the fascinating markets of China. We bought lots of fun souvenirs for the kids at home and lots of souvenirs for Wen and Wu to cherish as they grew older. Our court date and adoption finalization went off without a hitch, and our immigration appointment was completed easily.

The flight home was interesting. We thought the boys would sleep most of the way home, but nope, not a bit. They were fascinated by the television for a while but then they got bored. Every time they began to fuss or want to get out of their seats, the stewardess would bring them candy to settle them. I tried to explain that this was rewarding them for their behaviors, but she was more concerned with keeping them quiet so they didn't disturb other passengers. She just kept bringing them candy, which made them more wound up. It was a long flight, but we finally landed in Chicago. We were so happy to see the kids and to be home.

Introducing the kids to Wen and Wu is such a great memory of mine! Everyone was crying, hugging, and wanting to carry them around, and they brought immediate joy into our home. God knew our home needed some joy after the pain we had experienced with our dear Brian.

Wen and Wu did have some surprises for us, especially Wen. Neither boy was toilet-trained when we brought them home, so that was one of our first tasks. Wu toilet trained easily, but Wen did not. Months went by, and not one time did Wen pee in the toilet. Finally, one day I witnessed him peeing in the bathtub, but it was not coming from where it was supposed to. After a referral to a urologist, we discovered that Wen had a condition called hypospadias. His case was severe. He actually urinated from an opening near his testicles. Wen has had four surgeries to repair this condition and will need at least one more as he gets older. Remarkably, he handled all of his procedures with a smile—he even named his temporary catheter, Stevie. He is an amazing, resilient child.

Wu had a less severe case of hypospadias, which was corrected with one minor surgery. They both are severely allergic to animals. Can you only imagine if we had brought them home to the farm? Once again, God directed our paths, and even though giving up our farm was hard, God knew these boys would suffer there.

At one point, Wen and Wu appeared in a video that was distributed in China. Their birth parents recognized them and contacted us through the producer of the video. They were overjoyed to know that their boys were thriving and loved in the United States. We found out that the people featured in the orphanage photos with the twins were their birth parents, who had visited them frequently in the orphanage. They loved them deeply but knew that in China, their birth defects would prevent them from getting an education, having a career, and possibly even being able to marry. Any difference in China is very taboo.

We also found out their parents had purchased the outfits the boys were wearing when we met them, and they had followed us through Guangzhou as we pushed the twins in their strollers. We now have a great long-distance relationship with them, sending photos and videos to them frequently. One day, we hope to return to China with the boys so they can meet these people who gave them life. Some people would feel threatened but this, but Dale and I are not at all. We have always felt that no child can ever have too many people who love them and want them to succeed.

Wen and Wu make everyone smile! They have such charisma. They are totally devoted to each other and are inseparable. They have such compassion, are incredibly smart, and love helping mommy and daddy with anything. So many people have come to love these boys. Dale set up a YouTube channel for them, and now they create videos about everything from hand differences to their new hairless guinea pig. It's called Wen and Wu Tube, and people are constantly asking us to upload more videos. It has been a lot of fun! We cannot imagine our lives without these little guys and are very blessed and honored that God chose us to be their parents.

192

Take time to play, mom;
The laundry will wait.
Candy Land's starting;
You mustn't be late.
It isn't too hot, mom;
Go out and play ball!
So what if the laundry's
Piled all down the hall.
Find a good book
And then read it out loud.
Forget that the dryer lint
Is forming a cloud.
Folding? Forget it!
There's a game we must play.
There just aren't enough hours
In a mom's day!
Laundry is forever,
Children are not.
So, don't put laundry
In your playtime spot!

Chapter 21

Traveling Miles to Miles

Having a child with thalassemia was not difficult, but it did require frequent medical appointments. MengYan needed blood transfusions every two–three weeks and had numerous specialists monitoring her condition. She also needed yearly testing at the St. Jude Children's Research Hospital in Memphis. It didn't take long before her thalassemia became just another part of our life, another part of who we are as a family.

To keep up-to-date with the latest medical news regarding thalassemia, I joined a Facebook support group for thalassemia moms. We called ourselves the Thal Thugs because we often had to be pushy and insistent to get our kids the care they needed. Through this group, I became aware of a young boy who was in desperate need of a family.

Miles Xin Dai was thirteen years old. He had a form of thalassemia that was similar to MengYan's, but not quite as severe. He lived in an orphanage in southern China and needed to be adopted before his fourteenth birthday. Chinese law dictates that no child may be adopted after the age of fourteen. In fact, some orphanages release the orphans at the age of fourteen, even though they are completely unprepared for adult life. Most are uneducated and lack social skills, and many have health concerns for which they could never afford to receive treatment.

For Miles, being released from the orphanage at the age of fourteen would be a death sentence. He would have no way to afford the medical care required to sustain his life. Every momma in my support group advocated for this boy and prayed a family would rescue him in time.

We began to advocate for Miles and our hearts broke as we read about his life history. Found abandoned at a train station at the age of seven, he was brought to the orphanage and had been living there ever since. **Seven**. He would have remembered his parents! He would have been so scared to be alone in that train station. He would have had such pain and trauma from the very idea that the people who birthed him and loved him had just left him alone and scared. In my heart, I hoped and prayed that he could understand and forgive his birth family.

195

In China, medical care is not simple. I believe his parents could not afford the high costs of his transfusions and instead of watching him die slowly from lack of care, chose to leave him and hope that he would be found and cared for. I cannot imagine the heartbreak and helplessness they must have felt.

From reading his file, we learned that he was quiet and shy but loved to paint, create art projects, and enjoy music. He was small. Despite his age, he was wearing a boys' size 7/8 and weighed less than fifty pounds. We prayed for Miles every day, and I shared his photo and information with anyone I thought might be interested. I think people got sick of hearing about Mr. Miles.

A family from my children's school contacted me, and we talked at length about what Miles would need and how the entire adoption process worked. They were very interested in adopting Miles. This family decided to move forward with adopting him, and we were elated. We pledged our time and resources to help them fundraise to cover the cost of his adoption, and they began to complete the necessary mounds of paperwork. After a few weeks, we were devastated to hear that they changed their minds. They had a daughter with some significant health issues and were concerned that it would be too much for them to parent two children with ongoing medical needs. Miles, once again, needed a family.

Things were getting desperate. Any family who decided to adopt Miles would need to commit quickly and start paperwork immediately in order to complete his adoption before his fourteenth birthday. We watched as several families showed interest and then disappeared. Most families who choose to adopt are seeking a younger child and prefer to adopt a girl. There weren't many people looking for a teenage boy with ongoing medical needs. Time ticked by.

One evening, during our family devotions, Dale said exactly what I was thinking. **We** needed to go rescue that boy! He was running out of time. We knew how to meet his medical needs, as we already had a wonderful team of doctors who would love to care for another McKinney. We had the space for another child. We could raise the money, and we certainly had enough love in our family to love one more. Yes, it was crazy to bring home a fourteenth child, but we felt God moving on our hearts once again and being obedient to God is the thing Dale and I strive for most in our family. Let the paperwork begin.

We caught a lot of grief when we announced to the world that we were adopting Miles. There were some dear friends who were excited for us and overjoyed for Miles, but there were also those who thought we had lost our minds on this one. We heard horror stories about how bringing an almost fourteen-year-old boy into our home with younger girls would be a disaster. We heard about how adopting out of birth order would be devastating for our boys, even though we had done it already several times. We heard about how we were taking time and resources away from our other children by bringing home this boy. And, of course, the favorite saying that we have heard hundreds of times: "You cannot save them all."

Dale and I shut our ears to the voices of the world, to those who did not even try to understand our hearts. We listened to the voice of God who was telling us that this orphaned boy needed us, and we moved forward. But it was difficult. Going against the advice of people you love and respect is just plain hard.

While most (but not all) of our previous support system shied away from this adoption, God sent us His generous, understanding, and radical people. Total strangers stepped up to help us bring Miles home. The adoption agency reduced its fees to the bare minimum, while Miles' orphanage reduced their fees as well. Someone we had never met paid for our airfare to and from China. Our Thalassemia Facebook group donated funds towards Miles' adoption on a regular basis and supported our fundraisers. My dear friend Carol must have sold a thousand Subway cards as a fundraiser, and my dear mother made American Girl doll clothes non-stop for months just to help us with the adoption fees.

As we moved through the adoption process, we received more grants and assistance with Miles' adoption than any previously. This was confirmation to us that we were hearing God's voice accurately. I think it was the quickest and easiest we ever raised the necessary funds for an adoption. Miles' adoption was also the swiftest we had ever completed. Because he was very sick and aging out of the adoption program, both China and our government agreed to expedite his adoption. Our agency was lightning fast as well. Normal international adoptions from China take nine-twelve months, but we received travel approval from China in just under four months!

I think it was the week before we left for China that my faith wavered. Those negative voices I had fought not to hear began to creep back to me. I worried. What if this boy was difficult? What if he didn't want to be adopted? What if he was mean? Or cruel? What if he never bonded with us after the traumatic way he came to be an orphan? What if we got him home and there were additional undisclosed issues that we were not prepared for? Dale was once again my rock during this time, reminding me that our trust was in God. China, here we come again!

Miles was small, and he was scared. He was wearing nice new clothes, and as soon as he met us, he wanted to play a song for us on his recorder. He smelled like China, which was getting to be a familiar smell to me. His hair was so shiny and black, and his skin was tan, much darker than MengYan's or the twins'. His ayi's loved him and spent a lot of time reassuring him that this was a good thing and that he shouldn't be frightened. He came with us willingly. Even though his eyes looked fearful, he was so brave. I hugged him and together we walked out to our taxi and headed to the hotel.

Adopting an older child who doesn't speak English is challenging. Google Translate quickly became our best friend. We did get a chuckle, however, over some of the weird translations it came up with. It was so good to be able to communicate with Miles, letting him know our plans for the day and learning more about him.

Miles loved to eat and had quite an appetite. He especially loved these little stinky fish that were soaked in hot sauce. We could find them at almost every little food stand in China. He devoured them, and after he was done, we could literally feel the heat coming off his head. We went to a variety of restaurants, and he had a wonderful time trying new and different foods. He hated sub sandwiches, despised onions, and tolerated french fries. Breakfast was his favorite because our hotel had a huge breakfast buffet where he could try many different foods, both Chinese and American, and eat as much as he wanted. I think the boy gained ten pounds that week.

During our adoption interview, the notary asked us how many children we had. We explained to him that Miles was our fourteenth child. He could not believe what he was hearing and asked us why we would do such a thing. I looked at Dale, and he simply said to me, "Be bold." So, I told this notary about how we served Jesus Christ. I told him that we choose to obey God's Word and that many, many times, God commands us to care for the orphans. He asked me to write down these scriptures.

My mind was racing. I knew this could cause us trouble. I also knew that God gave Dale and me the opportunity to share the gospel with this notary. I wrote down many scriptures on a piece of paper and handed it to him. We were not sure if this man was genuinely curious or if this was a trap of some sort. The Chinese government is anti-Christian, and adoptive families are advised not to mention their faith. As our adoption was approved and we left the building, Dale and I looked over our shoulders all the way to the taxi. We were expecting to be followed and questioned, but that never happened. This man must have genuinely been curious. We committed to pray for him, hoping that maybe we had planted a seed.

Another amazing experience happened when Dale and Miles were talking through Google Translate. Dale was asking Miles if he had ever heard of Jesus. Miles acknowledged that people had come into his orphanage and told the kids there about Jesus. Dale had a great opportunity to share Christ with Miles in our hotel that afternoon, and even better, he found the Jesus movie in Mandarin, which they watched together. Miles and Dale were bonding well. Miles was a great kid, and all my fears and concerns melted away. Miles was meant to be part of our family; that was evident right away.

Miles' health was poor. We had his hemoglobin checked in China, and while it was stable enough for him to fly home without a transfusion, he was not feeling well. Several times he passed out, especially when we walked for long distances. Every time we drove through high traffic areas, Miles became carsick and vomited. He was pale and grew tired easily. His belly was large and hard, just like MengYan's had been. We needed to get him home.

The flight home was rough. Miles was sick most of the way home, and when we landed at the airport, he was too ill to walk. We were able to get a wheelchair and wheeled him through Customs and out of the airport. Ah, back in the United States! My dear friend Michelle met us at the airport, waiting with balloons and candy. What a blessing!

Miles was excited once we got to our home. He met all of his new siblings and his new dogs, and he loved his new room. He slept for almost twenty-four hours straight, and the following Monday, we took him to Peoria to see our beloved doctors at the St. Jude Midwest Affiliate. Dr. Saving, Dr. Ross, and DeeDee welcomed our boy with hugs and gifts. He was the star of the clinic.

As suspected, Miles needed many transfusions to get his red blood cell count to a safe level. His liver iron content was very high, but remarkably, he was healthy otherwise. His large spleen/belly began to shrink over time as his transfusions became more regular and his diet and care improved. Miles did have some complications such as gallstones and an inflamed appendix, which were removed. He had very damaged veins, so we attempted to place a port in his chest for transfusions, but after many infections, it had to be removed. He has very brittle bones and has suffered a few arm and shoulder fractures, so his physical activity is limited, but overall, he is doing great.

Miles is a wonderful boy. He loves to cook and is quite proficient at it. Nothing makes me happier than when he asks if he can cook dinner for the family. He gets along well with his siblings, tries his best in school, and is extremely creative. He loves to repair things, paint, and learn magic tricks.

Miles misses his friends in China very much. We are excited to take him back to China soon to visit his orphanage, friends, and ayis. He has, however, had his share of struggles. Life for an older child in the orphanage often involves stealing and hoarding to get what you need. This has proven to be a hard habit to break, even though all his needs are met now. Each day brings progress and healing.

Once, Miles lost track of me in a store. I heard him screaming and ran to him, thinking he had gotten hurt. He was not hurt, but instead, he thought I had chosen to leave him. I explained to him that I would **never** leave him; he was stuck with me. He responded that he never thought his birth mother would leave him, either. That brought me to absolute tears, and we both sat on the floor of Sam's Club, holding each other and sobbing.

Miles is my son, and I am forever grateful. I thank our Lord for helping Dale and me close our ears to the naysayers. I thank Him for giving us the courage and the motivation to step out in faith and make Miles a part of our family. Miles was meant to be with us. I truly believe that the minute he was born (or probably before), God already knew he was my son.

And just like that, there was one less orphan in the world and one more very loved son!

We've never held you
In our arms,
But you've won our hearts
With your boyish charm.
You've never seen us
Or heard our name,
But we still love you
Just the same.
We cannot wait
To bring you home;
We promise you
Won't be alone.
We have so much
Love to share;
You are an answer
To our prayer.
To see you smile
Is such a pleasure;
Miles, my son,
You are a treasure!

Chapter 22

The Return of Ronan AKA Bryson

Do you remember Rory's twin brother, Ronan? His story with us did not end when he went back with his birth mother. Every single night after Ronan left us, we prayed for that sweet babe. I prayed a selfish prayer that he would return to us. I wanted Rory to grow up with his twin brother, but I knew in my heart that God had a purpose for our loss. I just really wanted Him to explain it to me.

During the first few years after Ronan left us, I would call DCFS about once a month just to be sure he wasn't in the care of the state of Illinois. I always left my name and number, reminding them that I was momma to his full sibling so they would call me first if he ever came into their care.

We didn't hear much at all from Tae after she signed parental surrenders for Rory. The phone number I had for her was disconnected, so I didn't have a way to contact her. Kirsten and Greta also had no contact with her. And then one afternoon, when Rory was almost one year old, she called and wanted to see him.

We met at her home for what turned out to be a short, rather awkward visit to celebrate the boys' first birthday. It was great to see him, and yet, at the same time, it was heartbreaking. We were surprised to learn that Tae had changed Ronan's name, and he was now called Bryson. He was delayed in his motor skills as compared to Rory and was not walking yet. He and Rory didn't seem to know each other at all. I had this crazy idea that they would instantly recognize each other, but that did not happen.

When the boys were four, she called again, and this time we met at the indoor playground of a large church in Champaign. We had prepared Rory to meet his brother again, and he was excited!

"How long before we get there?" Rory kept asking.
"You're so excited, aren't you? We'll be there soon."

As soon as Rory spotted Bryson, he ran to give him a hug. Just as Rory was putting his arms around him, Bryson flipped out and punched Rory in the chest. Rory was devastated.

"I'm so sorry," Tae said. "For some reason, Bryson does not like to be hugged or touched, or even be held. He's also not talking."

In spite of all that, we had a nice visit. Thankfully, it was much less awkward than the previous one.

Seeing Bryson's ongoing issues, Dale and I suspected autism. That would also, in part, explain how difficult he was when he was a newborn infant.

There were a few more visits throughout the years, with Bryson and Tae visiting our farm. He fell in love with one of my guinea pigs, so we let him take the piggy home. With each visit, Bryson seemed to improve. He began to speak and to relax around us. Rory longed for a better relationship with him, but it was still quite difficult for Bryson.

The twins, Wen and Wu, had been home with us just a few months when we received a random phone call from Tae.

"Hi Ann, this is Tae, Bryson's mom," she said tentatively.

"Hi, Tae, how are you and Bryson doing?"

"Well, Bryson is doing pretty good, but honestly, I'm not. The truth is, I'm struggling, and I was wondering whether you would be able to keep Bryson for a few months while I work some things out. "

"Oh, wow, that sounds amazing. We would love to have him stay with us!" I couldn't believe what I was hearing. We had waited eleven years for this phone call.

"The doctor did diagnose him with autism, and I'm warning you, Bryson can be difficult. It won't be easy."

"Please bring him! We'd love to have him stay with us."

Dale cried when I told him that Bryson was coming to stay with us; actually, all of us cried. And then we rushed out to find him a bed. We had fourteen children at this point, with eleven of them still living in our home. Keagan, Brittany, Brianna, Bronwyn, Toby, Miles, Meng, Rory, Daley, Wen, and Wu. And now Bryson.

We met Tae at her home but then had to travel a bit further to have temporary guardianship documents notarized. She sent Bryson to our home with his clothing, his Nerf guns, and a few other toys. He was nervous but also excited. Rory hugged him a million times on the way home. Tae and I agreed to have frequent contact and that she would let us know when she was ready for Bryson to return.

Bryson and Rory did not look much alike, but they did have similar mannerisms. They liked red meat, especially steak, and they loved McDonalds. They enjoyed Nerf guns, video games, and being outdoors. Seeing them together again after all this time was so amazing.

Bryson had always been the youngest child in his home. He was very used to getting what he wanted, eating what he wanted, and spending as much time playing games on the computer as he wanted. He never had a stable father figure in his life and simply did not know what to do with Dale. He had a lot of trouble accepting Dale as an authority figure.

But Bryson was sweet, and he was quirky. He loved to draw and was very good at it. He especially loved to draw logos. When he was happy with me, he would draw me the SHELL logo, or the logo from an automobile. He knew cars and could tell you all the facts about the different models and engines. He was incredibly smart.

211

Bryson struggled with the chaos and busy-ness of our home, it agitated him. He was very intolerant of younger children and the noise they created. Wen and Wu drove him crazy with their constant chatter and activity, and Daley's frequent fussing bothered him. He struggled with the food we ate and the schedule we kept. Everything was so new and different for him. He rebelled, and he was difficult. We all tried so hard.

Rory struggled as well. At first, he tried to make his brother behave. He tried to teach him how things were in our family, but then he got frustrated and even angry. He could not understand why Bryson did the things he did. Autism is just really hard, harder than I ever realized.

We employed a family counselor, and all of us went to counseling sessions, trying to find ways to gain control of our stressful household. It was a rough time, a sad time. Things were so very different than what we had expected. But regardless of the struggle, I did love that little Bryson boy! There were a lot of happy times, when we did have fun together and could find a way to make a connection with him.

When I realized that things were beginning to be too stressful for Bryson, I let Tae know of our struggles. She decided it would be best to take him back home. It was heartbreaking to lose him again, but we were humbled by the fact that we didn't really know how to parent Bryson. Our family was one huge trigger for him, and there was nothing we could do to change that.

I always thought we could make any child feel welcomed and loved, but Bryson made me realize this was not true. Everything about us made him uncomfortable. His momma loved him and knew what he needed, so we packed him up and then we all cried, except Bryson. He was very excited to see his mom and be back in his quiet, calm home without the constant activity all around him.

When Tae arrived at our house to reclaim Bryson, Rory instantly noticed her baby belly. She was pregnant with another set of boy twins. She told us she had no clue what she was going to do—she knew Bryson would struggle with having newborn babies in their household. We prayed with her and offered to help her in any way we could. Poor Momma Tae; she needed strength and wisdom, so we would try to be her strength.

213

Bryson, we love you so very much, and we are sorry for the stress we caused you. We are sorry for trying to make you fit into a home that was so challenging for you. You will always hold a piece of our hearts. You are loved, you are special, and God has big plans for your life!

Those who truly seek Him,
May find Him in the least likely place….
In meeting the needs of a child.

Chapter 23

Micah and Matthew

After Bryson left our home and returned to his birth mother, we kept in touch with her. We wanted to be available to help her in any way with Bryson and the unborn twins. We were excited for her and hoped we would have the opportunity to meet them. Their father had moved in with Tae to help her care for the boys, and he was not quite as receptive to us as she was.

Tae let us know when the twins were born. There were no surprises; both were healthy and doing well. When they were about four months old, she called and asked if we would be willing to keep them for the weekend, as she was struggling to find childcare for them. Every child in our house was whooping and hollering with excitement! We met Tae halfway between our homes and loaded those precious babes into our van.

Their names were Micah and Matthew, and they were adorable. They looked nothing alike. Micah had soft, thin hair and was lighter-skinned. Matthew had a crazy, wild head of hair, a huge mischievous smile, and dimples. They also had very different personalities. Micah was reserved, cautious, and concerned. Matthew loved everyone and everything.

We ended up keeping them for several months while Tae worked out some childcare and personal issues. We had an absolute blast teaching them to play, feeding them, rocking them, and loving on those sweet babies. Getting them on a sleep and feeding schedule was a wee bit challenging, but even that didn't take as long as I expected. The girls all got a crash course on mothering, but it was actually Toby and Rory who surprised me. They helped out with every aspect of the twin's care. They were learning to be great daddies!

We were all sad when they went back home to Tae, but it was not a surprise. We were thankful that we were able to help her in her need. Getting to know and love Micah and Matthew was a blessing. We miss you, little bugs; please don't ever forget us!

Little hungry baby boys,
It's time to eat, put down your toys.
How about an apple, juicy sweet?

Grapes would make a tasty treat.
Green beans, carrots, or some peas?
Plums that came straight from our trees?
Fresh strawberries, a melon slice?
Oh, it all just sounds so nice!
Before you take that first big bite,
Stop and pray with all your might.
Thank God for his love for you,
And for his wonderful garden too!

Chapter 24

Sunny Danielle

Not long after we adopted Brittany, Brianna, and Brian, a sweet young lady by the name of Sunny came into our lives. Sunny and Brittany became close friends after meeting at church, and Sunny spent quite a bit of time at our home.

Sunny was a beautiful girl, a very special girl who touched my heart the first time we met and continues to do so. Sunny was born too early and spent months in the NICU, experiencing some brain injuries from her premature birth. She had cerebral palsy, which affected her lower limbs, making walking difficult and running impossible. However, it did not affect her mind, and she was incredibly smart, with beautiful blonde hair and big blue eyes. She reminded me very much of my Daley Faith.

Sunny and Brittany shared a lot of happy, crazy times. They were so very good for each other. They both came from dysfunctional families and had both suffered from trauma and neglect. So, in a way, they were therapy for each other.

Sunny's mother battled several addictions, which affected her ability to care for her children. Sunny grew up with various father figures in and out of her life and not much stability. Like Brittany, she did an excellent job of caring for her younger siblings and had assumed the mother role. I was so proud of her. She was able to run her household, maintain excellent grades, and get herself and her brother to church whenever the doors were open. She was a treasure. After her high school graduation, she enrolled in and completed a year at Greenville College, which made us even more proud.

One evening, during summer break, Sunny called. She was crying. She had gotten into an argument with her mother, and it had turned physical. She was hurt. Her mother had not only hit her with her fists but had also thrown her down a flight of stairs, hit her with ceramic flowerpots, and dragged her into the street in an attempt to have her hit by a car. Sunny's younger brother was able to reach her and drag her to safety. He then called the police, and Sunny's mother had been arrested.

Sunny- hysterical, traumatized, and terrified, was at the hospital being treated for significant injuries. She needed us, and we were honored that she trusted us enough to seek help from us. Our hearts broke over what Sunny had endured.

Sunny moved in with us the following day. She was a mess, both physically and emotionally. Her body was bruised and bloodied. There were police interviews throughout the day, as well as domestic violence counselors in and out of our home to check in on Sunny. She, however, just wanted to be left alone and forget what had happened.

We loved on Sunny and did our best to help her. She was so totally broken and lost. A young girl needs to feel that her mother is her support, her best friend, her ally. Instead, Sunny felt total betrayal and abandonment. To make matters worse, most of her extended family were angry with her for involving the police. They wanted the situation to be handled privately, as any abuse in the past had been. But this situation was very different; Sunny could have easily been killed.

Throughout this entire ordeal, Sunny grew closer to us and to the Lord. She began to heal and to realize that she was worthy of love, and we watched her continue to blossom and grow. We accompanied her to her court cases and frequent meetings with her lawyer. In the end, Sunny's mother agreed to a plea bargain and received probation, mandatory substance abuse counseling, and supervision. Sunny did not want to see her mother sentenced to prison, so she was happy. She deeply loved her mother, despite everything that had happened.

Sunny took a semester off of college to heal and recover. She then applied to the work-study program at the College of the Ozarks and was immediately accepted. We helped her gather the things she would need to get settled in, and off she went to college.

We are so proud to be a part of Sunny's world. She is so inspiring. She overcame her disability and a childhood of abuse and neglect and flourished at college as a stable, intelligent, and motivated adult. Sunny planned to become a counselor and will be excellent in this field, as she has been on the other side of counseling and therapy for much of her life.

Sunny is going to change the world. She is not our legally adopted daughter, but in the hearts of our family, she is! We are excited for her future, and in a strange way, we are thankful for her past. It made her who she is today and brought her into our lives. We love you, Sunny-bear, our beautiful overcomer! Rise, child, rise, and be who God created you to be!

Sunny, always know:
You have ENOUGH.
You do ENOUGH.
You are ENOUGH.
God made you perfect;
He takes joy in you!
He created you with great purpose!
Stand strong and carry on,
And we will always be here to support you.

Chapter 25

TEDDY

The first time I saw Teddy was pretty uneventful. It was when Dale and I were in China to adopt MengYan. Teddy was new to Shepherd's Field and had arrived there just a few months earlier. He was medically fragile, and what I remember most about seeing him for the first time was his pale, thin body and the look of discomfort on his face. In my mind, I said a quick prayer for this child, asking God to sustain him and bring him joy. I believe he was about two years old at that time.

Once we returned to the US, I kind of forgot about little Ted. Our days were consumed with getting MengYan healthy, helping her adjust, and getting her accustomed to being in a family with (at that time) seven children. My life as a busy mom kept Teddy in the back of my mind for over a year, until one day, I came across his photo on the orphanage website. Teddy needed a sponsor.

I read through the available information regarding Teddy, which confirmed that he was delayed both physically and developmentally. The doctors in China believed that he had a genetic syndrome of some sort, but no formal testing had been done. Something about those dark, sad eyes spoke to my heart. He looked so uncomfortable, almost as if he was in pain. My heart broke for him, and I regretted not spending some time with him in China. I printed out his photo, posted it on the door in our homeschool room, and our family began praying for him every single day. His photo hung on that door for many years.

When we began sponsoring Teddy, he was almost five years old. Each month we sent money to Shepherd's Field to provide him with the specialized care he needed, and every few months, we received an update on his health. Sadly, each update was about the same. Teddy did not advance developmentally and eating and gaining weight continued to be a struggle. He functioned in a manner very similar to that of a newborn child. He could not sit up, hold up his head or even move his arms and legs much. And he didn't smile, not in one single photo—there was always that grimaced look. We continued to pray for Teddy every day.

Throughout the years, we continued to sponsor Teddy. Several times I inquired as to whether Teddy would ever be adopted. I was told that his home orphanage considered him "unadoptable" and therefore, an adoption file had never been prepared for him. They also told me that if a family committed to adopting him, a file could be prepared. And then I was asked if **our** family was interested in making that commitment. Our family had continued to grow through adoption, but we were not convinced that we were meant to be Teddy's family, at least not at this point. But God had different plans.

In June of 2016, I received a new update on Teddy. I was shocked; he looked like a skeleton. I knew I had to do something, or the next update I would receive would be announcing Teddy's death. I was not about to allow that to happen, so I gathered a few dear friends and MengYan, and we headed back to China, armed with nutritional supplements, a wheelchair, and diapers.

Seeing Teddy face-to-face was terrifying. He was so frail, and he hated being held. He had smelly little rotten teeth. He was not only thin, but he was also sick and ran a low-grade fever the entire time we visited. But I did get a small glimpse of his personality. On the third day of our visit, we took some of the kids out for fresh air, and I placed Teddy in his new wheelchair. Being out in the sunshine seemed to lift his spirits, and low and behold, he began to smile. Once or twice I even heard a small giggle. I think it was at this point where I realized that I loved this child; he needed me, and I loved him. Now what?

By this time, we were parents to fourteen children: Brogan, Patrick, Keagan, Brownyn, Tobin, Rory, MengYan, Daley Faith, Brittany, Brianna, Brian, Wen, Wu, and Miles. Of these children, ten still lived in our home. How on earth would I convince Dale that we should adopt Teddy, knowing that he would need us for everything forever? It would be like having another Daley, a child who needed full care for every little thing every single day. My prayers changed drastically with this trip. Now I was not only praying for Teddy's health, but I was praying that God would allow me to be his mother.

After returning home, my first step was to ask Teddy's home orphanage to prepare his file. I had to agree to pursue his adoption, but that was not enough for them. They simply could not believe that anyone would adopt Teddy. I offered to pay for the costs associated with preparing his adoption file, and they quickly agreed. It was $80. It would take six to nine months for his adoption file to be available.

Soon afterward, Dale and I began to talk seriously about Teddy. My sweet husband loves Jesus, and he loves children. But, as you already know, he was father to fourteen children, including children with prenatal drug and alcohol exposure, blood disorders, autism, limb differences, and spastic paraplegia cerebral palsy. We carried a heavy load of parenthood, and Dale was not convinced that we could carry any more.

It terrified me also, but God had already placed Teddy in my heart, and I knew there was no going back. Dale put his complete faith and trust in both God and me and agreed to pursue Teddy as our son since I felt God calling us to this. So, we waited for his file to become available, and we kept praying that God would sustain Teddy's life while we waited. At this point, Teddy was nine years old and weighed sixteen pounds, a living skeleton.

And then it happened; Teddy's file appeared on China's shared list of available children. I asked my adoption agency to accept his file, and together we began to see if any families might be interested in Teddy. I knew in my heart he was ours, but our agency wanted to give other families the opportunity to learn about Teddy.

After many months, not a single family had requested his file, so we moved forward. Almost immediately, our first setback arose. Our previous home study agency blatantly refused to approve us for Teddy; they felt his needs were too great for us. We put together an appeal letter, backed by additional references and even support from our family physician. Still, the answer was no, but we didn't give up.

Through a fellow adoptive momma, a wonderful friend named Donna, God led us to an amazing new home study agency. They heard our story (which brought them all to tears), got 100 percent behind us, and quickly helped us leap through the paperwork process to begin Teddy's adoption.

Teddy was down to fourteen pounds by this point, so we were racing against time. My poor son had waited **so** long for us. We requested that his adoption be expedited for medical reasons, and our expedite was granted. So, instead of the normal nine-month wait time, we were looking at about four months. Finally, all of our documents were in China, and we were simply waiting for their approval. Every morning I woke up and immediately checked my email, waiting for that letter.

A letter did come, but it was not the approval. It was a letter from the CCWA informing all adoptive families that their new policy was not to approve any family with more than five children. I cannot tell you how devastated I was. I don't remember ever crying so hard in my life. I had to figure out how to tell Dale and the kids, as they would also be devastated. But God knew Teddy needed us, we needed him, and God moves mountains.

About an hour after this email arrived, I received a call from our caseworker. His voice quivered as he told me that China **had** approved our adoption literally hours before this new family size rule went into effect, and they had assured him that our adoption would be completed with no issues. God is so good!

Time flew by, and soon we were on the plane, heading to China. I was excited, and Dale was a nervous wreck. Despite all of our flights to China and Haiti throughout the years, he still didn't travel well, and he was nervous about meeting Teddy. I think he was still having some concerns about what our family was getting into regarding Teddy's care. I prayed all the way to China that Dale would love Teddy like I did, and that Teddy would accept our love and care.

We arrived at Shepherd's Field in the early afternoon and headed to Samaritans House, where Teddy stayed. There were several other children in his room, all severely disabled, and our sweet Teddy lay on a bouncy seat in the middle of the room. I'm sure we overwhelmed him. I picked him up and tried to hug and snuggle him, but just like last time, he hated it. He was so frail. Even holding him, I felt like I was hurting him. Dale held him. We both wanted to cry when we felt his poor sweet bones and saw the look of anguish on his face.

The ayi came and showed us how to feed him, but it horrified me. She laid him flat on his back and started spooning large bites of food into his mouth. He gagged, coughed, and sputtered with each bite. The act of eating caused him huge stress, and he was dripping with sweat by the time he was done. I do believe his nanny loved him, but she just didn't know a different way to help him eat, and she had very limited time to feed him.

Once we left Shepherd's Field, we were totally on our own with Teddy. Seeing him undressed for the first time was overwhelming; he looked like a child from the holocaust. We quickly discovered, however, that he was ticklish and he **loved** car rides. The crazier the ride, the more he liked it. He also, for some reason, enjoyed riding elevators.

And oh, how he loved to eat. We had fun figuring out what he could eat and how best to feed him. He loved congee, a fish paste type of soup. He also loved baked beans and oatmeal. We found that he could eat well if the food was the consistency of baby food, but he struggled with any sort of liquid. We ended up giving him a high-calorie protein supplement through a syringe, giving him one milliliter at a time. He quickly learned to take his liquids this way. We were a spectacle everywhere we went, as people in China rarely see Americans, and certainly not Americans feeding an emaciated child with a syringe.

Things went very well in China until the fifth night. We put Teddy to bed as usual, but about an hour afterward, we heard him fussing and thrashing around in his bed. He was sweaty, his arms and legs were pumping like we had never seen before, and he appeared to be in pain. He had a faint, weak cry. He had no fever, no injuries, and no reason for pain that we could assess. Dale realized this might be a weird type of seizure, based on the rhythmic movement of his hands and eyes. Daley has seizures, so this was familiar territory, but this was certainly a different type than what we were comfortable with.

We stroked his little head and sang to him, and eventually, the spasm stopped. He fell asleep. But it sure made me worry. We had been praising God for the wonderful trip so far, but now we turned to prayers for our boy. We realized that we were not out of the woods yet. A few calls and emails led us to a new concern: Refeeding syndrome. This can occur when a person has been starved or unable to digest nutrition for long periods of time. and one of the first symptoms is a seizure. Very often, refeeding syndrome is fatal.

Early the next morning, we contacted our Chinese guide and made arrangements for Teddy to have some laboratory tests to see if he did indeed have refeeding syndrome. I was a frantic mom as we waited for the office to call us with an appointment. We couldn't lose him, not after all of his years of waiting for us; we had to get him home.

Four needle pokes later, the blood was submitted for testing and Ted-man was back to his jolly little self. His smiles seemed to come easier each day. He seemed to be recognizing us, learning basic words, and understanding things much better than we expected. And it actually seemed like he was filling out a tiny bit, even though it had only been a few days.

The test results were good news; there was no hint of refeeding syndrome, praise God. The remainder of our time in China was spent getting to know this sweet treasure, shopping, and trying out new foods and new experiences. We did have another close call as a crazy driver decided to try to squeeze his car through a narrow road, putting his tires on the sidewalk and hitting Teddy's wheelchair. It was terrifying! Teddy was not hurt—in fact, he laughed hysterically. The wheelchair, however, suffered a fatal blow, with one wheel completely destroyed. We spent the rest of the trip tilting it up, so the broken front wheel did not scrape the road.

Overall, it was a great trip, and I loved getting to spend so much time with Dale, even with Teddy as a tagalong. Being parents to fifteen children is both a blessing and a struggle. It is hard to find time to remember that we are a married couple, very much in love, very much overloaded with life. It was good!

Upon our return, the entire family met Teddy at our front door, and he didn't seem to be overwhelmed by them. He laughed, giggled, smiled, and studied each one as if already trying to remember them. He instantly fell in love with MengYan and still adores her to this day. I sometimes think he believes she is his momma. They do both have those beautiful Chinese eyes, tanned skin, and shiny, jet-black hair.

Teddy is doing amazingly well. He came home at age ten wearing size eighteen months clothing but quickly increased in both size and weight. His official diagnosis is Pelizaeus Merzbacher Disease, which is an incurable, genetic form of Leukodystrophy. It can be progressive, but to date, he is still making gains.

Teddy attended school and learned to communicate through a program that allowed him to make choices based on pictures. He has favorite toys like BeatBo and Howard Parish, the dog puppet. He loves to be outdoors and enjoys peanut butter and jelly sandwiches. He gained some function in his arms and legs but is still unable to sit up or walk. Even though children with this diagnosis do not talk, I promise you I have heard him say Momma several times, and yes, it made me cry!

Regarding Teddy, I do have huge regrets. I regret not bringing him home sooner. I regret not seeing the beauty and value in his precious life the moment I saw him. I regret not praying for him more as he languished in his crib in China. I regret that I cannot assure his birthparents that he is loved. But mostly, I am thankful. God granted me my heart's desire and made me Teddy's momma and granted Teddy his heart's desire by giving him a family! This child is a treasure, and he has brought us joy. Welcome to your new life, Teddy; welcome to the **family**!

Little Bed-Head Ted,
I love your smile.
I love your crooked teeth;
I love your dancing eyes
And fidgety arms.
I see love in your gaze;
I feel God in your touch.
I am SO overjoyed
That God chose ME
To be your momma!

Chapter 26

Walking Through the Valley

On December 15, 2019, my precious Daley Faith met Jesus face-to-face. Her world became amazing that day as she was cradled in the arms of her Creator. Her broken body was made whole. No more curved spine, no more painful, dislocated hips, no more seizures. On the other hand, my world got dark. Even knowing where Daley was and the joy she was experiencing did not stop my heart from breaking. My arms became so empty. My days became so lonely.

Looking back over 2019, I should have noticed the slow and steady decline in Daley's health. In March, she awoke one morning and refused to open her eyes. Her behavior was normal all day long, but she would not open her eyes.

The following day was the same. I called several of her doctors, but none of them had any ideas about why she would refuse to open her eyes. The third day was different. Not only would she not open her eyes, but she was also grinding her teeth. I knew what this meant for Daley. It meant she was in pain. We loaded up in my old, rickety van (my kids fondly call it the Trash Can) and headed to the emergency department of St. John's Hospital.

A few tests later, and Daley's neurosurgeon was called in for a consultation. Everyone suspected the VP shunt in her head was failing. This would allow spinal fluid to build up in her head, creating pressure, pain, and, eventually, death. Dr. Satchivi confirmed this diagnosis, and two hours after we walked in the doors, Daley Faith was being prepped for surgery. It was terrifying.

Dr. Satchivi was a very professional, kind, and caring man. He replaced Daley's shunt and did an excellent job of calming my nerves at the same time. We were able to be with her in the recovery room almost immediately. She woke smiling and happy, not appearing to be in any pain at all. I was shocked to see my beautiful princess missing half of her gorgeous blond hair, which the nurse handed to me in a plastic bag.

Daley recovered so quickly that she was only hospitalized overnight, so we took her home the following afternoon. The first thing I did when we returned home was to shave off the rest of her hair. It just made sense to me to let it all grow back together to the same length. So now my sweet girl was a baldy. She was happy to be home, as she dislikes hospitals. Having her siblings fawn over her was exactly what she wanted and needed.

About a week after her surgery, we noticed her head swelling. It felt squishy and spongy. A quick trip to Dr. Satchivi confirmed that she had a spinal fluid leak under her incision. So now, my sweet bald girl had to have her head wrapped as tightly as possible. This worked very well, and within a few days, her head returned to normal.

Another week passed, and Daley began to run a low-grade temperature. Her incision was red and angry—another trip to see Dr. Satchivi revealed an infection in her incision. Thankfully, it was at the wound surface only and had not gotten into the shunt itself or into her brain tissue. A skin scraping and a few weeks-worth of antibiotics and Daley was, once again, back to her happy, recovering self.

Another setback happened just a few weeks later. Daley quit peeing. She would go an entire day without urinating, which made her extremely uncomfortable and agitated. This time we set off to see Dr. Matthews, our beloved urologist who treated Wen and Wu for their hypospadias. Daley was diagnosed with neurogenic bladder; her brain was no longer telling her bladder to empty.

Daley now had a urine catheter, which needed to be emptied and flushed several times a day. A few months of this was overwhelming, so we decided to have a supra-pubic catheter placed surgically in Daley's abdomen. This allowed us to empty her bladder whenever she did not do it on her own. It was much easier than the catheter she had previously, and we quickly got used to this new medical care our girl required.

Throughout the summer, Daley struggled. She got pneumonia several times. She contracted urinary tract infections frequently, despite how careful we were with her supra-pubic tube. She also started something new and frightening; autonomic storming. This is an ugly little episode, which is not medically explainable. Her heart rate would go sky-high, her blood pressure would plummet, and her oxygen levels would crash. There is no way to stop this event, so supporting her during these storms was our only recourse. We put oxygen on her to sustain her levels and prayed, sang, and snuggled her through them. They were scary, ugly, and so overwhelming. Every time she stormed I had a real fear of losing her.

I was worried about losing Daley. I wondered what it would be like. I wondered if I could even handle it emotionally. I worried about walking the kids through the death of a sibling. Little by little, I felt God bringing this to my mind. I know He was preparing me. Dale and I had met with a palliative care team, and we wrote medical directives for Daley's care. We knew what we did and did not want done for our girl in the event of a crisis. We needed these things in writing so that if and when the time came, we could fall back on the decisions we had made when we were thinking clearly.

We prayed that if and when we did lose Daley, God would grant us two things: We wanted her to be at home with her family, and we wanted it to be natural. We did not want to have to make hard decisions, such as removing her life support. We feared that if we had to make that type of decision, we would second-guess it for years to come.

On December 7, 2019, we received news that Gabby had passed away at St. Louis

Children's Hospital. She was twenty years old. Gabby is the princess who won my heart and made me comfortable with adopting a medically fragile child. Hearing of Gabby's death rocked me hard, as I felt in my heart that God was using Gabby's death to prepare me for losing Daley, just as He used her to prepare me for her arrival.

As a family, we mourned Gabby's death, but it allowed us to talk about how that would look for us. One entire night of family devotions was dedicated to talking about Gabby and how impossible it was to prepare for such a tragedy even when you know it is in the future. We just didn't know how close that future was.

On December 10, Daley was junky. We suspected pneumonia, and a quick trip to Dr. Wall confirmed that she did have fluid in her lungs. Our normal protocol was to give her a Rocephin injection daily for three days, and in every single instance of Daley having pneumonia, this had been successful. So, she got an injection three days in a row. This worked like a charm, and on day four, our girl was clear. The following day she was back to her baseline, smiling, watching her favorite shows, and fussy when daddy walked by in an attempt to get him to snuggle her.

On Sunday, December 15, I awoke at 7:00 am. I checked on Daley and found her sleeping peacefully. I took a quick shower, dressed for church, and then headed downstairs to start her morning routine. I called out to her and she did not stir, which was very unusual. When I looked down at her, her face was ashen. I touched her and realized she was gone. I yelled for Dale. He somehow knew, and immediately cried out in grief. He rolled her over and began doing CPR compressions. I pulled back his arm and reminded him that we agreed not to resuscitate her.

At this point, we were both crying. We didn't know what to do. I asked Dale to bring her to me, and I sat in our favorite chair, the chair where we snuggled, the chair where I fed her and gave her the daily medications she needed. He brought Daley to me, and I snuggled her close. She was still warm. She smelled like the cherry blossom lotion I had lathered her in the evening before. I wept and rocked in that chair, holding my baby. I kissed her hair and her beautiful face.

I faintly remember hearing Dale make several phone calls. And then I heard each child cry out, as Dale woke them up and told them one by one. Bronwyn wailed so loud the

242

house shook. Rory immediately began kicking or punching something. The twins came and sat at my feet, crying.

Soon the paramedics arrived. They needed to verify that she had no pulse or heartbeat. And then my living room began to fill with all sorts of people, mostly police officers. I didn't know that when a child dies in their home, it is automatically considered a criminal investigation until the juvenile detective or coroner declares the death natural. I sat holding my lifeless child, sobbing, surrounded by well-meaning but incredibly awkward police officers. It was horrible.

And then God blessed me in a way that had never happened before and hasn't happened since. As I held Daley, I was still weeping softly, and I heard a low, deep moaning. I realized that it was coming from **me**! It was long and low, and several of the officers glanced at me curiously, so I know they heard it also. I could not stop it or control it in any way. The moaning stopped momentarily and then began again, both frightening and beautiful at the same time. When the second moan ended, I felt a warm, perfect peace come over me. I looked down at my baby and realized that it was not her anymore. My baby was in the arms of Jesus! It wasn't until a few days later that I found the scripture that describes my experience.

Romans 8:26-27 (NIV)

In the same way, the Spirit helps us in our weakness. We do not know what we ought to pray for, but the Spirit Himself intercedes for us through wordless groans. And He who searches our hearts knows the mind of the Spirit, because the Spirit intercedes for God's people in accordance with the will of God.

The next few days were a flurry of activity. So many people were in and out of our house. I don't think we have ever had so much food delivered to us, and many people called, texted, and stopped by to see if we needed anything. Friends we had not seen for years reached out to us. We felt love from every direction. So many people became the hands and feet of Jesus as they ministered to our family.

Planning Daley's Celebration of Life service was easier than I had expected. We chose to have a small, short, informal service at a funeral home just a few blocks from our home. Someone anonymously paid every single dime of the expense. We had a two-hour visitation directly before the service. So many people came to show their support and love for our family that those two hours seemed to drag on for ten hours. I mustered up the strength and poise to read Daley's chapter from this book to the people who stayed for the service, and then Dale shared an amazing message. Dale spoke about Paul and Silas and how they were imprisoned during an earthquake. That earthquake freed them from their prison cell.

Acts 16:26 (NIV)

Suddenly there was such a violent earthquake that the foundations of the prison were shaken. At once all of the prison doors flew open, and everyone's chains came loose.

He related that story to Daley Faith being a prisoner in her broken body, and how her earthquake came the minute she died and was given her new, perfect body. Her earthquake gave her a freedom and a love greater than she had ever experienced. After his message, two of Bronwyn's friends, George and Adrianna, sang *WayMaker*. It was beautiful.

Here is Daley's obituary:
Daley Faith McKinney met Jesus on Sunday, December 15, at 7:30 am.

She leaves behind a family who cherished and adored her.
Parents: Dale and Ann McKinney,
Siblings: Brogan (and Zachary) New of Texas, Patrick McKinney, Keagan McKinney, Brittany McKinney, Brianna McKinney, Bronwyn McKinney, Tobin McKinney, Brian McKinney, Miles McKinney, MengYan McKinney, Rory McKinney, Teddy McKinney, twins Wen and Wu McKinney, Timothy Owens, Sunny Welker.
Grandparents: Cecil and Marcia Aldridge, Jiggs and Ginger McKinney, Betty Smull, nephew Landon, many wonderful aunts and uncles and dozens of cousins.
And of course her beloved nurse, Sandy Delaughter.
She also leaves behind her first family: Tom and Chrissie Flynn and brothers Aiden and Kellen.

Daley Faith was a treasure, a beautiful soul, and she was a blessing to everyone she met. She brought pure joy to the McKinney family, and the love of God could always be felt through her.
Although she will be missed dearly, we know she is now free from her disabilities and made whole in Christ Jesus. Hallelujah!

Visitation will be Thursday, December 19, 3-5 pm, at Brintlinger and Earl Funeral Home, 2827 N. Oakland Ave., Decatur, IL, followed by a casual memorial service presented by Daley's family.

Memorials to In His Hands Orphans Outreach, PO Box 425, Rochester, IL 62562, to be used specifically to help families adopt children with disabilities. Please be generous. There are 132 million children in our world who do not have the love of a family

After everything was over, I had to resume my life. My life without Daley Faith, who had consumed so much of my daily activities. For the first few weeks, I got up each morning and went straight to her bed to check on her. And if that wasn't bad enough, I would then go straight to her medication station to begin making her morning meds. Habits are hard to break. Loading only one wheelchair into the van made me feel awful each time it happened. It was even hard to say Teddy's name without also saying Daley's, as those two were always paired up in my conversations. My house was just one big reminder of my girl.

I still miss Daley so very much. But slowly, God is healing my broken heart. It took some time for me to begin to thank God. I thank Him for choosing me to be her momma; it was such a privilege. I thank God for giving me ten years with her instead of the one year the doctors had predicted. I thank God for letting her die peacefully, sleeping in her own bed, surrounded by all of her favorite toys, and even wearing her favorite pajamas.

I thank God that He didn't require us to make hard decisions, decisions that we might have second-guessed for years to come. I thank God that He used losing Daley to repair and rekindle many relationships in my life, including restoring my relationship with my sister, Amy. And I thank God that He used Daley's death to make my family stronger, closer, and more appreciative of every single minute we have together. God is a good Father.

Today we said, "See you soon" to our beautiful baby. There aren't any words I could say to explain how much Daley meant to us. From the moment they brought her to us, we were so in love. Being Daley's siblings meant using her crying at the top of her lungs to always find where mom was at in Walmart. Acknowledging that no matter who was younger than her, she was always the baby of the house, the princess. It meant learning how to feed her through a G tube and comforting her through seizures.

Also, if you're caught staring at Daley, you're caught staring at all of us. And we're very protective, so we will also kindly educate you on how to treat our sister. For Wen and Wu, it meant turning on their ambulance sirens and rushing to Daley every time she had a seizure (which is more often than you might think). For the older kids, it was knowing that she was blind, so we would sneak up on her as quiet as possible and yell, "BOO!" She would jump out of her socks and either smile or get very annoyed.

For Keagan, it meant knowing she was very sensitive to touch, so he would blow and blow on her face until her face was so scrunched up she couldn't take it, she would laugh so hard. It meant getting mad at mom for suggesting a babysitter when we wanted our baby with us. It also meant watching the **same** *sesame street episode every single day.*

For the girls, it was spending so long doing her hair up pretty just for a few pictures before Daley drooled all in it. For all of us, it was noticing when people acknowledged everyone in the room except her. We talked to her like a normal, regular person, because she was. It was our joy to make every adjustment to our lives that we did; we didn't even notice, because we loved her. She was the best little sister we could've ever asked for, and going back, we wouldn't change a thing about her.

Daley, thank you for bringing so much joy to our lives. Thank you for always adjusting to the chaos, sitting through all the basketball games, and letting us spoil and fight over you. Thank you for the laughing and happy fits; we needed them more than you think. The castle is so lonely without the princess—we just miss you. We love you so much, sissy.

Written by Bronwyn McKinney

Chapter 27

It's Your Turn!

This is our story, the story of the amazing children who have blessed our family and given Dale and me purpose. I honestly think it all began the moment God pricked my heart with the idea of adoption when my friend Michele died, leaving behind a newborn son. I pray that through this story, God will prick your heart and you will consider adoption, foster care, or orphan care. Children are in need all over our world. I challenge you to look up the latest statistics on orphans; it will devastate you. Better yet, do a YouTube search for an amazing video called *Hope is Fading*. It will wreck you. But it's truth.

If you are wondering if God wants you to get involved with a child who is not yours biologically, just read His Word. He has commanded us in many places to care for the orphans. He doesn't want them to be left alone. He wants them set into families. God created the family unit, and it pleases Him.

The most beautiful thing about adoption is that God first adopted us. He set that example for us. He adopted us into His family even though we were troubled, difficult, disobedient, and obstinate. Even though we were sick or had physical challenges. He saw past those things and saw us for who He created us to be. Now He asks us to do the same. He asks us to trust Him and take that step toward that child who needs us.

I encourage you to do some digging. Inquire about foster care in your community. Google international adoption and learn as much as you can. Reach out to adoption attorneys and crisis pregnancy centers in your state to see if they have a need that you can meet. Make a difference with your life by making a difference in the life of a child. Or if all these things seem overwhelming or impossible for you, then find a foster family or adoptive family and ask them what you can do for them.

I know first-hand that many such families could just use a few hours "off" or a gift card for the local ice cream parlor. It means more than you can imagine just for someone to notice and care. Another great idea is to become a "Big Brother" or "Big Sister" to a child in the foster care system or become a CASA volunteer. Every child needs to have love and support from as many angles as possible, especially a child who has endured trauma or displacement.

Together, we can build amazing families and put a dent in the orphan crisis. Together, we can change the world, one child at a time. **Nothing would make me happier than if my story was not unique, but instead, it was common**. Can you even imagine?!

Epilogue

So, you may be wondering what our plans are? We "think" we are done adopting. My adoption advocate colleagues have flooded us with files of waiting children, but we are allowing time for our hearts to heal before we consider adopting again. God has put us on standby for the moment.

But, on the other hand, I have always hated odd numbers.
And there's
Always Room for More!

About The Author

Ann McKinney and her husband, Dale, are parents to 15 children, 13 of them through domestic and international adoption. Ann is a team leader and board member with In His Hands Orphan Outreach (Inhishands.org) and also serves as the Haiti Team Coordinator where she manages trips to the IHH Orphan Home in Grand Savanne, Haiti. She was the original founder and director of Treasured Adoption Foundation, where she helped dozens of orphaned children find forever families. She has devoted her life to advocating for orphans and vulnerable children and enjoys sharing her experience through speaking engagements and conferences.

Made in the USA
Monee, IL
09 May 2021

68004781R00154